Endors

Franchising without Fear is a necessary guidebook for making an educated decision on buying a business and choosing a franchise. Fear often gets in the way of making the final decision of starting a business or buying a franchise. This book explains how to deal with the fear by taking a methodical approach to this life-changing decision through knowledge and preparation.

—Kary Oberbrunner, author of
Day Job to Dream Job and *Elixir Project*

Franchising without Fear is a much needed guidebook to the knowledge needed to make an educated decision on the franchise that is right for you. Fear often gets in the way of making the final decision of starting a business or buying a franchise. Trish uses her many years of experience as an accomplished Franchise Broker and Multi Unit Franchise Owner to walk her readers through how to deal with fear by taking a methodical approach to this life—changing decision. This is a must read for anyone considering purchasing a franchise.

—Charles Grosse,
CGMG Enterprises, LLC

Susan – Thank you.

Trish Benedek

Franchising
without Fear

Franchising without Fear

Six Steps to Successfully Buying your Own Business

TRISH BENEDIK

AUTHOR ACADEMY elite

Published by Author Academy Elite
P. O. Box 43
Powell, OH 43035

www.AuthorAcademyElite.com

Paperback ISBN: 978-1-64085-447-5
Hardcover ISBN: 978-1-64085-448-2
EBook ISBN: 978-1-64085-449-9
Library of Congress Control Number: 2018957559

Visit the author's website at www.trishbenedik.com

DEDICATION

This book is dedicated to my father, Russell Pennock, who ingrained the entrepreneurial spirit in me from a young age and helped me see endless possibilities.

Never underestimate the power of dreams and the influence of the human spirit. We are all the same in this notion: The potential for greatness lives within each of us.

—Wilma Rudolph,
First American Woman to Win
Three Gold Medals at the Olympics

CONTENTS

LIST OF TABLES

If you want something in your life you have never had, you will have to do something you have never done.

—Unknown

INTRODUCTION

As a serial entrepreneur, I remember dreaming of owning a business from the time I was a young girl. Growing up, my dad owned a construction business, and for a long time, I just assumed *everyone's* dad had his own business! Over the years, I watched him struggle, juggle, and triumph as a small business owner. It all made me wish to one day become part of his company, however, my father died when I was young and the business was dissolved.

My father still served as an inspiration for me. Over the years, I not only worked in the corporate world, but I have owned several businesses, including a retail gift shop, a wholesale basket business, and a horse training business. Throughout my life, I have always had the desire to help people learn about business and lifelong education. My experiences as a career technical educator and the master's degree I attained in Workforce Development and Education while working full-time have been an important part of achieving this goal.

Now as a franchise consultant, I have the rewarding experience of helping people find the venture or franchise that is right for *them*. My desire to help others shows in the most recent acquisition of a fundraising franchise. Through this business, I help schools, churches, civic groups, and non-profits raise needed funds for their important work.

I am writing this book because I know what it is like to be in your shoes. I have experienced stress and frustration in the corporate world and often felt I was in the wrong field. I have been laid off, downsized, underemployed, and treated as a number rather than a person. I have had the motivation and desire to own a business yet not been sure where to turn for reliable advice on where to get started. When I first went looking for a franchise, I was not familiar with the nuances of the franchising model. This is the kind of book I wish had been available to me at that time.

Growing up in a family business, I am familiar with the sacrifices made by all family members. As an experienced business owner who started from scratch, I have conducted all operations of a business. During my time as a franchise coach and consultant, I have spoken to hundreds of people interested in owning a business and have guided people through the process of choosing a business.

Surprisingly, I have discovered that the most significant obstacle to starting a business is not money, time, kids, or anything similar. It's *fear*. If you're like most entrepreneurs, you hold many fears about starting a business. They include the fear of what will happen, the fear of what won't happen, and the fear of moving forward. I am writing this book to help you work through your fear and find your dreams.

Inside this Book

This book contains several sections that address different aspects of buying a business or franchise. I start with addressing your current life situation in which something is not right in your career, and then I walk you through confronting your roadblocks and fears about owning a business. Step three addresses what franchising is and choosing a business model. In Step four I present your blueprint for selecting a franchise. Towards the end of the book, I include important decision-making tools to help you make informed decisions. Finally, in Step six we cover some of the nuts-and-bolts for getting your business off the ground.

- Step One – Why?
- Step Two – Confront your Fear
- Step Three – Why franchising?
- Step Four – Selecting a Franchise
- Step Five – Making a decision
- Step Six – Running Your Business

If you're still sitting in a corporate office stewing over how things are run, then your future business is only a dream. You're taking an important first step by reading this book. Arming yourself with knowledge, preparing for your business venture, and moving forward is the way to realize your dream.

So, stop dreaming and start doing! If you have the desire to own your own business, then you need to do it. There is no time like the present to pursue your dreams!

There is a certain amount of dissatisfaction that goes with knowing your time, talent, and abilities are not being properly used.

—Zig Ziglar

STEP ONE

WHY?

ARE YOU DISSATISFIED?

If you are dissatisfied with your job, you are not alone. According to a Gallop poll released in 2017, eighty-five percent of workers worldwide admit to hating their jobs.[1]

Have you been downsized, laid off, let go, and made obsolete? Are you underemployed, without a clear path to move up in your company? Perhaps you are just tired of the same grind day in and day out. Do you ask yourself—why?

Corporate refugees are those who were forced out of a "real job" or got fed up and quit. Some individuals wish someone would fire them because they don't have the courage to quit. Talk to a corporate refugee long enough, and you'll find they think of themselves more like *escapees*—and they love their new-found freedom.

In my work with individuals looking to buy a franchise, I have talked to many people in the above circumstances. Their frustration is apparent from our first conversation.

Trapped, lack of control, no passion, disengaged

One factor that is sure to motivate someone to make a change is feeling trapped in their current state. Nothing kills the spirit more than feeling trapped. Moreover, if the only way you can move is sideways or not at all, it may be better to leave altogether.

Are you frustrated by your lack of control? Do you regularly see things that need to be changed, yet lack the credentials to make changes? Are there improvements you would like to make, yet don't have the power to do so? Owning your own business will allow you the liberty to make improvements and give you more control over your destiny.

Are you in a position that is changing, and you are dreading a forced change? Perhaps you aren't interested in your work, you do not feel any passion for your career, and you're tired of making money for someone else. You are not engaged.

Entrepreneur at heart

Perhaps you are an entrepreneur at heart. In fact, according to UPS's Inside Small Business Survey, "Roughly two-thirds of people want to own their own business."[2] Dreaming of owning a business is very common, and if you are an entrepreneur at heart, your destiny is laid out for you. You probably think about it continually, dream about it at night, and plan for it in your head. I know from my own experiences, it is impossible to lose the entrepreneurial spirit within me. This book will help you identify options and take stock of your personal preferences so you can make an educated decision.

What if you cannot make the decision? If you are having difficulty deciding to buy a franchise or open a business, this book will give you concrete actions to help you make an educated rather than an emotional decision.

If you have been talking about your dream business to others, and you are starting to think about what it will look like, this book will help you put your plans on paper. On the other hand, if you are in the planning stages of your venture, there are valuable tips and strategies inside these pages.

Have you taken time to analyze what is missing in your life? What is stopping you from realizing your ambitions? How do you start to take action and make your dream a reality? How do you figure out where to begin?

This book will provide you with clear directions on the path to choosing the right business or franchise. Read on to discover a workable course of action that will pulverize the grind and turn it into stepping stones to success.

Leaving corporate life

The first phase in your consideration is to take stock of your motivations and make a choice. Whatever your reasons are, it is a good idea to take a long look at them to help you determine if turning your back on the corporate world is the right move for you.

Do you want to be the one to call the shots, make all the decisions, and do things your way? If so, owning your own business may be the solution, still, keep in mind that it's a tremendous responsibility to make every decision for your business. Often, individuals do not want to give up the security of a steady job or a long career.

As a business owner you gain more control over the time it takes to get things done. Since you are in charge, you set the deadlines and can knock things out when you want to. You won't need to wait for another department to send you the specifications. This flexibility is energizing for the entrepreneur.

Questions to ask yourself before starting a business

Before even considering owning a business or franchise, you should ask yourself serious questions about going into business for yourself. Before taking the plunge, consider the following attributes about yourself.

Are you a self-starter? Do you take the initiative to get things done? It will be you that follows through with details and gets work done. Your business success and employees depend on your actions to get and keep things moving.

Physical and emotional stamina. Owning a business is both mentally and physically demanding. You may need to work long hours and seven days a week, especially in the beginning stage. Do you have the physical and emotional stamina to run a business?

What is your purpose? Ask yourself why you want to do this and examine your values, talents, and passions to help you define your purpose. Will your business add value to others? What do you feel is your purpose? Answering this question will make it easier to focus on the right goals.

Take your family into account

In my house, I'm the boss; my wife is just the decision maker.

—Woody Allen

Contemplate how owning a business will affect you and your family. The first few years of new business can be challenging for family life. Talk with family members, tell them what to expect and ask for their support.

Keep Your Spouse or Partner in the Loop

I have worked with a few people who wanted to buy a franchise. However, they did not want to include their spouse or partner. One gentleman (I'll call him Joe) said he would figure out what franchise he wanted, then present it to his wife and talk her into it. I urged Joe to bring his wife along during the process because she is going to be part of this decision even if she is not actively working in the business. Joe refused to tell her. I presented Joe with some outstanding options for franchises that fit his profile. However, Joe never bought a franchise. I believe it was right around when he revealed his plans to his wife that he disappeared.

Would you buy a refrigerator or a car without the opinion of the other adult in the household? Why would anyone buy something such as a business without including their partner in the process? The family will be affected by the decision, the day-to-day operations, the time involved, and the financial aspects. Owning a business affects every part of your life. Be sure to involve the significant people in your life in the process.

If you spring the idea of such a significant change on your spouse or partner towards the end of the process, of course, he or she will be inclined to resist you. You're trying to suddenly convince them to upset the whole balance of your family life. Thus, it's essential to get their blessing *before* proceeding down this path. Otherwise, you may be wasting not only your time, but the time of the franchisor, and you'll be in for a big disappointment. Spousal/partner buy-in is paramount to your success and long-term familial happiness.

The important people in your life need to understand the commitment you are making. If they are enthused and supportive about the business the transition will go a lot smoother.

As a franchise consultant, I recommend the spouse or partner be in on the calls and discovery process. Bring your partner along for the ride, their support will go a long way in helping you make a great decision.

One fed-up corporate refugee

People have many reasons for wanting their own business. One gentleman said he was *fed up* with corporate life, had resigned from his position and planned to buy a franchise. He had enough of the day-to-day drudgery and wanted to help families in their community. We worked together to find the ideal franchise for him. Three years later he is doing well in his business and very happy with his choice. His company is thriving, and he has realized the dream of owning a business that gives him financial as well as personal satisfaction. This story repeats itself every day in the franchise world with people who want to leave their current occupation and start out on their own.

If your frustration and dissatisfaction are such that you can hardly get out of bed in the morning, then the best thing you can do for yourself is to explore better options. When you are researching your alternatives, you will be surprised at the possibilities that will emerge.

Throughout this book, we will explore possibilities and give you a blueprint to help you find the correct path.

VISION

No one is fated to work a dead-end, soul-killing job. You *can* create your own destiny. If you take stock of your motivations as a first step and realize that nothing would make you happier than being able to leave your current job, then it's time to move on to creating your vision. What is your vision? How do you picture your perfect business or career? Creating a journal and writing about your dream and your ideal business will go a long way to helping you picture your goal. As your dream becomes clearer, you'll be able to envision it, and having a picture of it in your mind will help it become a reality.

Let's look at some options for creating a destiny that will help you feel more in control of your future. There are thousands of books, articles, and resources related to finding your path. I encourage you to take the time to work through a few of those to expand your vision. For this book, I want to focus on the entrepreneurial track of opening a business or buying a franchise.

If you are considering opening a business or a franchise, there are endless possibilities. However, you should not merely go out and choose an enterprise or franchise haphazardly. Your personal goals and capabilities should be addressed thoroughly before making a choice.

Whichever path you choose, know that, if you want to be successful, you need to be willing to remain committed to your dream. There is a great deal of time and work involved in owning and running a business. Everyone starting a business has visions of happiness, success, and money in the bank. However, successful business ventures are successful for many reasons. Many factors are at play in owning a thriving business, and the most important is the hard work of the business owner. It's important to note that the only place success comes before work is in the dictionary!

In our dreams, we all aspire to do great things. Is it possible the only thing holding us back is fear?
—Jack Canfield

STEP TWO

CONFRONT YOUR FEAR

Ponder what Marianne Williamson is saying in this excerpt from her book *A Return to Love*:

Our deepest fear is not that we are inadequate. Our deepest fear is that we are powerful beyond measure. It is our light, not our darkness, that most frightens us. We ask ourselves, Who am I to be brilliant, gorgeous, talented, fabulous? Actually, who are you not to be? You are a child of God. Your playing small doesn't serve the world. There's nothing enlightened about shrinking so that other people won't feel insecure around you. We are all meant to shine, as children do. We were born to make manifest the glory of God that is within us. It's not just in some of us; it's in everyone. And as we let our own light shine, we unconsciously give other people permission to do the same. As we're liberated from our own fear, our presence automatically liberates others.[1]

It is a beautiful paragraph that you may have seen shared around the internet because the sentiments within strike a chord in each of us. Do not be afraid to let your light shine.

FEAR: FRIEND OR FOE?

Everything you always wanted is on the other side of fear.

—George Addair

Fear can be a friend or a foe. Because we do not like change, we become accustomed to the same routines and find changes unnerving. Our routines become comfortable. The fear of change can keep us stuck in the same day-to-day habits. The security of routines in our lives prevents us from moving forward and taking steps to make a change. When we work in a traditional job where we have a steady paycheck, health benefits, and paid vacation, we become comfortable with the security a job provides. Giving up this security is not easy. When you open a business, there are no guarantees, and you are giving up this safety. Arming yourself with knowledge and preparation are vital to dissipating the fear of change.

Fear is Primal

I have a great fear of snakes. I have a difficult time watching snakes even if they are on television. One day I was doing stretching exercises and looked up, and there was a rattler curled up on the floor, staring me down. I was petrified! I screamed, jumped up, and ran up the stairs. My heart was racing. My dog followed me up the steps—proudly carrying the snake with him!

In fact, the snake was dead. Moreover, you want to know the saddest part? *It was a taxidermy snake all along!* Even I was surprised at my fearful reaction. I did not want to touch it, so I left it there and made my husband pick it up when he returned home.

I tell you this ridiculous story to demonstrate that fear is a primary human emotion. After the snake incident, I was shaking, my heart was beating hard, and I was fearful. That was my nervous system kicking in and my basic instinct telling me to run to keep myself safe. Our nervous system is programmed with fear to survive. It is a primal survival instinct, and when we sense danger or feel unsafe, the instinct kicks in and fear takes over. Once I stopped and realized the snake wasn't real, I stopped shaking and was eventually able to return to normal. Armed with information, I was able to move on with my day. Survival plays a part in this primal fear. If our ancestors did not fear a lion, they would not have survived. Through trial and errors, they found out what to fear and what not to fear.

Amazingly, fear has a purpose

Fear is meant to protect us, to alert us to danger. Everyone feels fear; it is a warning and a caution sign, it tells us to act with care. We know fear is felt on different levels; it can be mild, medium, or intense. Each person feels fear in varying intensities. My husband is not at all afraid of snakes. He may have a slight concern yet not nearly as intense as mine. Fear can last a long time or for a brief period. It depends on the circumstances and the person involved.

Frequently, we let our fears block our progress because we always imagine worst-case scenarios. Our fears can keep us up at night or become nightmares. Theo Tsaousides, Ph.D., author of *Brainblocks, Overcoming the Seven Hidden Barriers to Success* writes,

> *Fear of failure is the intense worry you experience when you imagine all the horrible things that could happen if you failed to achieve a goal. The intense worry increases the odds of holding back or giving up. Being successful relies to a large extent on your ability to leverage fear.*[2]

The rest of this section will help you learn to leverage your fear and use it to help you make good decisions.

WHAT DO YOU FEAR MOST ABOUT STARTING A BUSINESS?

What do you fear the most about starting a business and buying a franchise? Is it the fear of failure? The fear of not having enough time to do the things you enjoy? Perhaps you feel you do not have the skills to run a business. It is helpful to thoughtfully take into account your concerns and address them before making a decision. In this book, I provide you with strategies to confront your fears and find ways to buy a franchise with confidence. Let me be clear: purchasing a franchise or starting a business is not for everyone. Nevertheless, if it is your dream and you have the right motivations, you can make it happen.

Worrying is normal

Worrying about what will happen is normal. We want things to go our way, and we want the best outcomes. Even so, worrying makes it challenging to concentrate and is exhausting. Worrying and concern about what might happen make it difficult to sleep, much less take necessary actions in your career and life.

Most of the time we don't want to face our fears, yet this is a mistake. We often fear things that cannot hurt us. Frederick Fabella puts it this way:

> *This [avoidance] is especially true of matters which we shouldn't fear. We become afraid of things that cannot harm us. However, we have to realize that whenever we fear something, we grant it power over us. And the more we avoid it, the worse the fear gets. In such a situation, we have to challenge our beliefs by facing our fear head-on. By so doing, we may prove to ourselves that there is nothing to fear.*[3]

If you continue to let the fear overpower you, it will become more challenging to overcome. You will find yourself doing less and less and bowing down to fear. You may live to regret your decisions and become one of those people that lives a life unfulfilled. Where would any of us be without taking risks? Would we fall the first time we walked and never get back up? How about riding a bike, taking a challenging class, going to college, or driving a car? I'm thankful some-one took the risk to learn to fly so I can fly to any destination. If Ray Kroc had not taken the chance to buy out the McDonald's, the company would not be the same today.

When we have a fear, it's about control. We fear losing control of what will happen. Frankly, we must face the fact that we can't control everything. Worrying will not guarantee a positive result, it will make things seem worse. Sometimes we need to be willing to accept whatever happens and let go. Let go of the worry, think positively, and move on.

Change and fear

Whenever you tackle something new, there is fear involved. When we are comfortable with our lives, we sometimes get stuck and don't make progress toward our pursuits. The first paragraph of this section addresses why we avoid making uncomfortable decisions. It is the fear of the unknown that paralyzes us, so the best preparation is to explore the unknown.

One way to work through our fear is to prepare for new endeavors with thorough knowledge and preparation. If you are reading this book, you may have realized that fear is stopping you from making an important decision about change in your life. Jack Canfield has written many books about building your confidence. He is aware that allowing fear to control our thoughts is detrimental to our health and well-being.

> *Fear erodes self-esteem, corrupts our self-confidence, and over time convinces us that we are losers.*
> —Jack Canfield – *Dare to Win*

If we are convinced we are losers, it will be difficult to succeed. It is important to realize that self-confidence and self-esteem are traits that lead to positive outcomes. No one wants to be a loser; awareness of the "fear factor" will go a long way in helping you win in the business world.

Fear can freeze you in your tracks—and you cannot move forward if you allow it to paralyze you. It is like a large boulder that gets in the way of progress. As you are looking for a business and working toward a decision, remind yourself *why* you want to make a change. Your reasons will help you keep the end goal in mind and push the boulder out of your path.

EFFECTIVE STRATEGIES FOR WORKING THROUGH FEAR

Fear is an emotion that can be thwarted by recognizing it for what it is. In this section, we will explore effective strategies for conquering the emotion that holds us back from moving toward our goals. Before you begin your search, the first strategy is to change your mindset from a negative outlook to a positive one.

Strategy 1: Transform your mindset

Make a conscious effort to think positive thoughts about this process.

First, you need to realize that fear is a regular part of the process. Everyone has fear and doubts when starting something new. We fear life changes such as buying a business, getting married, or having children. Anxiety is experienced when we begin a new job, go for a job interview, attend a networking event, or go to a new school. There is fear as you drive to a big game, and there is anxiety when you get out of the car and see the stadium. When purchasing a home, there is fear of financial commitment and worry about moving to a new location. It's part of our makeup to fear new events. Whether we admit it or not, changes bring fear of the unknown. Accordingly, if we all caved into our doubt, there would be no progress!

Remember, you are not alone. Everyone who has ever bought a franchise or started a business had reservations about their decision. Accept your fear, then make a conscious decision to change your mindset about it. "Switch from thinking about failures to thinking about discrepancies between what you hope to achieve and what you might achieve," says Tsaousides. "Discrepancies provide you with information that you can study, explain, and learn from so you can recalibrate your future efforts."[4]

We commonly find discrepancies between what we have read and what we already believe or our actual experiences. People love to find these kinds of little inconsistencies and use them as excuses not to move forward. The excuses become like sharp stones on bare feet, slowing you down. Friends and acquaintances often bring up reasons not to buy a franchise or business. Don't let their excuses or rocks become yours.

Emotions

Another mistake people make is letting their emotions get involved in the process. Think about the process as an educational opportunity. Invest in a franchise for the right reasons based on calm, clear, and rational thought.

Learn about the concepts and various choices you have before making any decision. Some of the best opportunities are not glamorous, nevertheless, they are still excellent money-making businesses. Leave the emotions behind and evaluate your business and lifestyle ambitions. Often emotions get in the way of making good choices.

> *Have no fear of perfection; you'll never reach it. Nothing in life is to be feared; it is only to be understood.*
> —Marie Curie

Strategy 2: Step Out of Your Comfort Zone

> *You never change your life until you step out of your comfort zone; change begins at the end of your comfort zone.*
> —Roy T. Bennett – *The Light in the Heart*

As we discussed in Step One, when someone is comfortable, it's almost impossible to make changes. If you have no aspirations to change, you will probably want to stay in your comfort zone. However, if you have higher expectations of owning your own business, you will need to change what you are doing. We've all heard the popular definition of insanity—to keep doing the same thing over and over and expect a different result. If going into work today kills a piece of your soul, what makes you think it will do anything different tomorrow?

People who start a business or buy a franchise have stepped out of their comfort zone, blasted through their fear, and climbed the mountain to accomplishment.

Strategy 3: Set Goals for Success

When you are contemplating a life change such as purchasing a business or franchise, goal setting is an integral part of the process. Establishing goals and objectives are a necessary part of making significant decisions. In Step four, I will detail specific strategies for setting the kind of goals that will lead to your success.

Strategy 4: Determine Your Road Blocks

> *Success, it is not the position where you are standing, but which direction you are going.*
> —Oliver Wendell Holmes

Be aware of the reasons you give for not fulfilling your goals. Often excuses are a way to deal with fear without admitting that it's even there, much less holding you back. In our culture, we do not want to admit we are afraid. We are afraid of embarrassing ourselves. Other people in our lives may be discouraging us from our business dreams. Fear keeps us from trying, and not trying makes it impossible to make progress. Not moving forward then becomes a self-fulfilling prophecy: If you don't take a step forward, you will never reach your targets.

Other blocks to moving forward with a business are feelings of inadequacy. Those voices in your head that say you can't do it. Realize that everyone has these feelings and that you need to put those voices out of your head and say, "I *can* do it."

Beware of imposter syndrome. In a 2018 blog in *Psychology Today*, Susan Weinschenk Ph.D. explains the Imposter Syndrome where an individual has difficulty internalizing their accomplishments and has a fear of being "exposed as a fraud...Despite evidence of competency, people with the imposter syndrome remain convinced they do not deserve the success they have achieved."[5] The Imposter Syndrome is more common than you realize. Think through a time when you were given an award, advancement, or grade and you felt you did not deserve it. You did earn it, however you let feelings of inadequacy tell you otherwise. Do not sell yourself short!

Fear of failure

Perhaps you have failed before and fear it will happen again. Consider this story about the famous inventor Thomas Edison. When asked about his thousands of failed attempts to create the light bulb, he said, "I have not failed. I've just found 10,000 ways that won't work."[6] We've all had learning experiences that didn't work the first time; we had to keep trying until it worked. To fear failing is to misunderstand the role of failure in success.

To accomplish great things, you will have to do new things, and failure is a part of business and life. Marie Forleo says, "Anyone who accomplishes great things in business and life is bound to 'fail' along the way. Feeling like a failure is a natural part of becoming a success. It's actually a good thing and means you're taking action and putting yourself out there."[7]

Identifying excuses you are using to stay stuck will go a long way in helping you work through your concerns and begin to step out of your comfort zone. By identifying your roadblocks in the beginning, you will help ensure they don't come up at the very end and derail your plans. Use Table 3 to help you determine your roadblocks.

> *When I dare to be powerful, to use my strength in the service of my vision, then it becomes less and less important whether I am afraid.*
> —Audre Lorde – *The Cancer Journals*

Strategy 5: Prepare with Knowledge

The best way to work through the fear is to manage your expectations with preparation. Most people fear to speak to a crowd. The best way to get over the fear of speaking is to prepare, practice, and then just do it. Learn as much as you can about yourself and the skills you bring to the table. Learn as much as possible about alternatives before making a choice. The more you know about the business/franchise, the more familiar you will feel. This knowledge will help reduce your anxiety and keep you focused on your ambitions.

Reflect on the type of lifestyle you desire and how the business will fit into your life.

Real and imaginary fear

Determine the difference between real and imaginary fear. We often imagine the worst that can happen. The fear is real, still we usually overestimate the threat to survival. The danger is a product of our imagination. Through study and preparation, the danger subsides, and you can learn how to avoid what you are afraid will happen.

Remain flexible

Think about what can happen and decide to remain flexible. Tsaousides notes, "Some goals require focus and persistence. Others, however, require openness and flexibility. Being able to reevaluate and redefine the outcome you hope to achieve is a good buffer against the fear of failure."[8]

Arm yourself with facts and positive outcomes

Build confidence by arming yourself with facts and a firm belief in a positive outcome. Elisa Boxer, journalist and mindfulness coach, says you should label your fear—admit that you are afraid. Then follow it up by asking your fear a simple question: "Are you here to keep me safe, or to keep me small?"[9] Is your fear keeping you from danger or is it preventing you from taking the risks you need to grow, keeping you small? Is it holding you back from crossing the creek to get to the other side?

When it comes to business, you'll find most of your fears are keeping you small and on the wrong side of the stream.

Strategy 6: Alleviate your Fear of Failure

People fear failure because they worry about the consequences.

According to Tsaousides, there are several adverse effects that people with a fear of failure expect. These include: "feelings of shame and embarrassment, a big blow to self-esteem, the prospect of an uncertain future, the loss of social influence, and disappointing important others."[10] It's interesting to note that people worry more about losing friends or losing face than losing money. Are you more worried about what people will think about your business than how your business will help you achieve your goals?

> *I've been absolutely terrified every minute of my life—and I've never let it keep me from doing a single thing I wanted to do.*
> —Georgia O'Keeffe

Ways to alleviate the fear of failure

To lessen the fear of failure, Tsaousides advises "you should identify the consequences of failing that scare you the most and evaluate your ability to deal with these consequences."[11] Change your focus from negative thoughts to building confidence in your ability to handle your concerns.

In other words, you *should* ponder the worst-case scenarios. That way you can decide what you would do if they happened, and by having a plan, you alleviate your fear. Ask yourself "What is the worst case scenario?" "Fear of loss is higher when it is limitless. Knowing the worst is survivable can ease this fear."[12]

Perhaps you fear you won't make as much money as you expected, or that the business will turn out to be more work than you thought. Do you have money to fall back on or someone who can help in a pinch? Most of the time when people complete this exercise, they realize that they *can* make it through stressful circumstances. It's helpful to recognize that most fears never materialize. We spend too much time worrying about "what ifs." Richard Kronick who wrote an article in the Huffington Post, *10 Powerful Ways Successful*

People Overcome Fear, advises, "The next time you find yourself overwhelmed by all the scary things that *might* happen, try bombarding your mind with positive and empowering thoughts and affirmations. Affirmations really do work, accordingly, they take time, practice, and persistence."[13]

Go ahead and allow yourself to identify your fears and worst-case scenarios. Have a plan for how you can work through your concerns. Then set aside those negative thoughts and focus on positive thoughts and outcomes. The ability to deal with the results of our choices is what makes us confident. Knowing that fear comes from *within* ourselves gives us the confidence of being able to deal with the outcome no matter what happens. Confidence will help you work through the fear. Talking about your fear will help you control your emotions toward it; the more you acknowledge the fear, the less it will control you. Your plan will alleviate the fears and make it easier to make the right decision. Your plan is another stepping-stone to the other side of the stream.

Strategy 7: Face Your Fears

> *I can accept failure; everyone fails at something. But I can't accept not trying.*
> —Michael Jordan

Think about a time when you were afraid to do something and pushed yourself through your fear and dived into the fray. What was the result? Were you relieved, happy, ecstatic? Was it worth pushing through the fear? Getting on the other side of fear has excellent benefits for your confidence and self-esteem.

Fear keeps us from taking action, however, the action is the means to conquer your anxiety. Have you known someone who was too fearful to perform in front of an audience? Performers have to step out of their comfort zone to move to the next level. Performers that face their fears realize it is worth momentary discomfort to take action. One of my close friends is a performer; let's call her Susan. Susan has performed for more than 35 years in front of crowds of people. Every time she goes in front of a crowd she is nervous, doesn't eat and does not want to engage in conversation. She has fear, and she knows it will happen every time.

Regardless, after beginning the performance, Susan finds herself getting into a flow and forgetting about the audience. The fear begins to disappear, and it's a little easier every time; she becomes more comfortable each time she performs. Susan knows there will always be some fear, and she also knows it helps keep her sharp. By standing up and facing her fear, she is now at another level on the ladder to success. If Susan did not take the opportunity, she would not be able to move forward—she would languish in the same spot.

After you prepare yourself, the best way to get rid of fear is to do the thing that you are afraid of. Arm yourself with knowledge, push yourself through the fear, and move onward. You will be glad you did. By arming yourself with knowledge about the opportunity you have chosen, you will find much of the fear will dissipate. You can never be 100% sure that things will work out—that is why they call an investment a "risk." There is always an element of risk. No one will give you a guarantee that you will make a certain amount of money, however, if you take the time to prepare and arm yourself with concrete facts and follow the steps in this book, your fear should be manageable.

Go for it!

In the book *Dare to Win*, Canfield explains that a friend taught them a technique for convincing yourself to move forward. Whenever you are trying to talk yourself out of something, "close your eyes and repeat the following, out loud like a Gregorian or Buddhist chant: 'Oh, what the heck, go for it anyway!' Repeat it again and again and again and take the right action to obtain the right result. Start by trembling if you must but start!"[14]

Someone who has never failed has never taken a risk. Owning a business is a challenging, exciting experience. If you don't take the chance, you will never get to experience the thrill of being your own boss. Embracing change is a significant portion of life and business. Those who don't embrace change will be left behind.

> *Confront your fears, and you can make them disappear.*
> —Napoleon Hill,
> *Think and Grow Rich*

Strategy 8: Anticipate Your Regrets

Just like everyone has fear, everyone has regrets. Think about things you've regretted in the past. How many of them involve *not* taking action? How many were actions you wish you hadn't taken? Now, which did you learn more from—the actions you took or the actions you didn't take?

I'd rather regret the things I've done than regret the things I haven't done.

—Lucille Ball

My guess is you, like most of us, learned more from taking the wrong action than from not taking any action. The same is true of your business. Think about what you will regret if you don't invest in yourself to open your dream business. If you stay in an uninspiring job, always dreaming of leaving, will you regret it? Will you wonder every day why you did not go ahead and pursue your secret ambitions? Will you go to bed at night dreading getting up in the morning and going to your awful job?

In my business, I often talk to people who say they wished they purchased a particular franchise twenty years ago. They feel they missed out on an excellent investment. The good news is that there will always be good business investments—new franchises are opening every day. Do not ruminate on the past; rather be optimistic about investing in the future. In twenty years other people may be looking at you and wishing they had invested in the same business.

Reduce your pain when you step out of your comfort zone and into the independence owning a business can give you. It is our problems that give us the opportunity to stretch ourselves and find strengths we did not even know we possessed.

Entertain the possibilities. Owning a successful business gives you financial freedom, flexible hours, the ability to help others, and a reason to be proud of your accomplishments. Would you regret wanting that more than wanting the "safe" option of doing nothing? Can you live your entire life not knowing what could have been?

I have learned over the years that when one's mind is made up, this diminishes fear; knowing what must be done does away with fear.

—Rosa Parks

Strategy 9: Make a Commitment

One of the potential franchisees I worked with (I will call him George), really wanted to buy a franchise. Together we went through the six-step process I will detail later, and we arrived at three options that were a good fit for his goals and lifestyle. Finances were not a problem, he had management experience, and he was motivated to move quickly. However, he was looking for the *perfect* business, and just like the *perfect* marriage, it does not exist. After perusing several solid options, George got tired of the dance and gave up. He did not take any of the concrete discovery steps that would lead him to confirmation of his choice. As far as I know, George still has not found a "suitable" business.

George's story is all too common. I understand his hesitation: choosing a business is not easy. There are so many choices, and it is hard to know where to start. People like George get overwhelmed by the options and wind up making no decision at all. I don't know if George is feeling regret, though, it's a good bet he is, and I don't want the same thing to happen to you.

Committing to overcoming your fear is paramount to moving forward. Without commitment, you will find all kinds of excuses not to make a change. The boulder will stay in your path, and it will be impossible to get to the other side. Your commitment will come with motivation and the motivation will carry you through.

Mareo McCracken, revenue leader at MoveMedical, describes what makes a commitment different than other kinds of choice: "Commitments are not decisions; commitments are not preferences, commitments are not ideals. They are stronger and deeper; they are steadfast and immovable. Once you commit to something, nothing else matters."[15]

When I was training and showing horses, I had to overcome many fears. I spent a great deal of time riding, taking lessons, caring for and conditioning my horses, reading about horses, and preparing for the shows. I always had intense fear when I was about to go out on the course to ride at the show. Once I was out on course my fear dissipated, my instincts took over, and I rode my horse with confidence. I was extremely committed to horse-back riding and showing. My actions of preparation helped eliminate the fear—I was focusing on something else besides the fear.

McCracken says, "Commitment always leads to confidence; it is a cycle. Action creates success and success will create confidence. If you don't have confidence, take action, and the confidence will come because you will find success because you will not be thinking about fear. All fear is neutralized when commitment is proven through action."[16]

By commitment through action, your brain neutralizes the fear.

Commit to realize your dreams. If you don't commit to the process, the preparation, and the education, it will be hard for you to make it happen. You will encounter many conscious and subconscious reasons to derail your plans. You will find many reasons not to buy that business or franchise if you let the negatives consume you and do not rely on the positives. Committing to make a change will take you a long way toward changing your life.

McCracken says, "Since our brains only can consciously focus on one thing at a time, once you are in the act of doing, your fear fades away. Therefore, taking action reduces conscious fear."[17]

Russell Simmons, entrepreneur, record producer, and author, is committed to his businesses. He has learned not to give up. He says, "Many of my biggest business endeavors were failures before they became a success. Some failed for as long as six years before they hit. Everyone around me thought I was crazy. You just have to stay at it."[18]

Russell Simmons's can-do attitude, hard work, and entrepreneurial spirit has helped him stay the course and now he is a multi-millionaire.

> *Most men lead lives of quiet desperation and go to the grave with the song still in them.*
> —Henry David Thoreau

Strategy 10: Imagine a Newer, Brighter Future.

There are reasons you are taking this journey. Refer to them often, so you don't slip back into old patterns and comfort. See yourself in the new position—leading your company into the future. Imagine the possibilities. Envision a happy future where things work out the way you planned.

Step in the doors of your new business, imagine having the ability to call the shots and grow this business from the ground up. In the morning, the alarm does not even ring, and you are up before it rings because you cannot wait to go to work and build the business. Imagine having enough equity in the business that in twenty years you can sell it and retire comfortably or leave it to your children. Consciously keep your dream alive every day as you make progress towards your vision.

If you want to conquer fear, don't sit at home and think about it. Go out and get busy.
—Dale Carnegie

STEP THREE

WHY FRANCHISING?

THE DEFINITION OF FRANCHISING

Let's look at the definition of franchising, how a franchise gets started, and a brief history of franchises. It is helpful to understand the difference between a franchisor and a franchisee since I will be discussing both throughout this book. According to the International Franchise Association (IFA),

- A **franchisor** is a person or company that grants the rights to others to do business using their business processes, brand, and trademarks.

- A **franchisee** is an individual or group who buys the rights to use the franchisor's trademarks, brand name, and systems.[1]

Equally important is to have a good understanding of the definition of a franchise and the impact franchising has on the economy.

According to the *Business Dictionary*, a franchise is,

*The arrangement where one party (the franchisor)
grants another party (the franchisee) the right to use
its trademark or trade-name as well as specific business systems and processes, to produce and market a
good or service according to individual specifications.*

In exchange for the rights to use the systems, trade
name, and processes, the franchisee typically pays a
one-time fee called a franchise fee plus royalties for
a specified percentage of sales revenues. The franchisee also "gains (1) immediate name recognition, (2)
tried and tested products, (3) standard building design
and décor, (4) detailed techniques in running and promoting the business, (5) training of employees, and
(6) ongoing help in improving and upgrading of the
products."[2]

In brief, then, the franchisor grants another party
(the franchisee) rights to use their business systems and
intellectual property for a fee. In exchange, the franchisee is granted the use of the franchiser trademark
or trade name and ongoing support and improvements
for a specified period. The franchisor expands the
business faster and with less capital than if they try
to increase development on their own. The franchisee
is provided with the opportunity to build and grow a
business and reap the benefits of the franchise.

How does a franchise get started?

A faster expansion is the driving force behind new
franchises. The majority of business franchises get
their start when the company is doing well and they
would like to expand. If the company sells a product or
service that is easily replicated, the industry could be
a good candidate for franchising. Expansion through

franchising is less costly than development by adding company units.

Once the franchise is set up, the business sells franchises to people that they feel will be a good fit for their brand. New franchisees have the rights to use their brand, trademarks, systems, and procedures in exchange for a royalty fee and other specifications spelled out in the franchise agreement. The franchisor assists the franchisee with start-up, as well as, training and ongoing support to run the business.

THE EVOLUTION OF FRANCHISES

The original definition of the word *franchise* is from late 13th century Old French and meant "freedom, exemption; right, privilege," from a variant stem of *franc, franche*, "free." By the 18th century, the meaning was narrowed to "particular legal privilege," meaning "authorization by a company to sell its products or services."[3]

This business meaning of franchises has not changed in hundreds of years. A franchise gives individuals autonomy and control to sell products and services they would not have otherwise had the rights to sell.

Interestingly, franchising as a business model has been around a lot longer than people realize. Many texts mention the Singer Sewing Machine Company as a pioneer of franchising. However, the origin has a much more remarkable story.

The following brief history draws heavily on the blog, "The History of Franchising," by Michael Seid, Managing Director of MSA Worldwide and co-author of *Franchising for Dummies*.

The ancient roots of franchising

Franchising growth has been driven over the years by three main factors:

1. The desire to expand territories and control the expansion. Expansion is controlled through agreements, licenses, and or charters.

2. Limits on capital, both human and financial. It is costly to expand, and through franchising, the franchisee provides the needed capital to open territories in other areas.

3. The need to overcome long distances. By having the franchisee open in other areas, the franchisor overcomes the long distance hurdle.

Franchising can be traced to the time when the early church was expanding and additionally was used as a method of government control. The first evidence of a type of franchising was before the middle Ages. Some historians believe that even the Roman Empire may have used franchising. There is evidence that franchising first appeared around 200 B.C. in China when rickshaw drivers were granted routes through protected territories.

1200–1562—Early Franchising

As far back as the Middle Ages (the 1400s), tax collectors made agreements with landowners. These arrangements were similar to franchises in that the tax collectors kept a percentage of the money collected and turned the rest over to the government.

In England and Europe, the king or queen owned all the lands and granted land rights to influential individuals (nobles) and the church. Those who held land rights (grants) were to protect the areas and were free to set tolls and collect taxes. A portion of the tolls and taxes were paid to the Crown. This early use of franchising—granting control, collecting fees, and paying a share of the payments to the king or queen—demonstrates the three driving forces of franchising: (1) desire for expansion and control over lands, (2) a limit on human and financial capital (the Crown could not be everywhere), and (3) overcoming long distances by placing individuals in charge of territories.

1492–1700 — Franchising in the Colonies

In 1492, Europeans discovered what they would call the New World, presenting new economic and international trading opportunities. Governments and private businesses used franchising to expand and control over great distances.

There are numerous examples of early "franchising" in the New World. In 1609, the Dutch East India Company contracted Captain Henry Hudson to explore the New World and find passages to Asia. On this voyage, Hudson discovered the Northeast Passage which gave the Dutch claims over the Hudson Valley in New York. The contract with Henry Hudson was an early form of franchising.

Other examples are charters granted in 1606 by King James I of England. This exclusive charter for Virginia was awarded to the London Company. Captain John Smith managed the first permanent British settlement in the New World, which was named Jamestown. In 1624 King James I revoked the charter and brought Virginia under British control. A great deal of the colonization by European and British powers was conducted under what we would now call "franchise relationships."

1731 — Benjamin Franklin was a Franchisor

Before the United States was born, Benjamin Franklin entered into several partnerships that meet the definition of franchises. In 1731, Franklin joined into a co-partnership with Thomas Whitmarsh to print and publish the *South-Carolina Gazette* and print Franklin's writings. There are records of many other co-partnerships with other printers. The income from Benjamin Franklin's franchised print shops allowed him to travel to France for long periods, thus giving him time to negotiate assistance from France in the Revolutionary War. The impact of Franklin's franchising is profound, as there may not have been the United States were it not for his franchised print shops.

1700's — Product/Commercial Franchising

In the 18th century, breweries used franchising to distribute their products. Tavern owners purchased all their alcohol from the breweries and received financial assistance in exchange. The taverns agreed to this single purchase arrangement to obtain financial assistance from the breweries. The single purchase arrangement was all the breweries required—they did not involve themselves in the daily operations of the business. This system is still in place. It operates similarly to a product or distribution franchise today.

1850 — Railroads and Franchising

Around 1876, the first restaurant chain was founded in the United States by Frederick Henry Harvey in a railroad terminal. The railroad wanted restaurants in depots for their customers, and they provided Harvey with locations in the stations. Within 11 years, there were 120 Harvey House locations along the 12,000-mile railroad line. Harvey wanted sound quality control and visited establishments regularly, creating an early oversight model similar to today's franchise or chain locations.

1891 — Martha Matilda Harper's First Franchise

Many of the business structures Martha Matilda Harper developed have become a part of the modern franchise system. She provided her franchisees with training, branded hair care products, field visits, advertising, group insurance, and motivation.

Ms. Harper started her salon business in 1888, licensed her first franchise in 1891, and grew to more than 500 salons and training schools. Her business continued through the 1900s to the 1960s and was acquired by a competitor in 1972.

1900s — Distribution Franchises

As an answer to the high cost of transportation, in 1901 Coca-Cola issued its first franchise to Georgia Coca-Cola Bottling Company. The cost of distributing beverages in glass bottles was prohibitive and kept the industry at the local level. By issuing franchises, Coca-Cola could ship the syrup to the local bottlers, and those bottlers could package and distribute it regionally. Coca-Cola retained control of the product quality and significantly expanded their markets. Coca-Cola is one of the first and most successful franchises in the United States.

1922 — Automobiles and Franchising

The drive-in restaurant was one of the early innovations inspired by automobiles after World War I. A&W Restaurant became the first drive-in franchise, driven by its A&W Root Beer beverage brand. A&W Root Beer was franchised in 1922, and the first A&W Restaurant opened in 1923. In 1924, owner Roy Allen wanted to expand, but he did not have the capital. His answer was to franchise the restaurants. Other restaurants that are part of this early innovation in franchising are White Castle (1921), Howard Johnson (1935), Kentucky Fried Chicken (1930), and Dairy Queen (1940).

The boom in franchising in the United States did not take place until after World War II. As the significant shift from an agricultural to an industrial economy took place, manufacturers granted licenses to individuals to sell their products. Products such as cars, trucks, paint, gasoline, and beverages were licensed to others to sell. These are product distribution franchises—the individuals are only required to sell the products as part of their business.

In the mid-1960's the franchising boom began and has flourished ever since. From the early print shops of Benjamin Franklin to the dealerships of General Motors and beyond, the U.S. has been touched and expanded by franchising.[4]

Franchising has come a long way from the early days and has expanded exponentially. Many positive changes have been made to benefit both the franchisor and the franchisee. Through franchising, thousands of people have realized the dream of owning a business.

KINDS OF FRANCHISES

As I've been describing, franchising is a method of doing business through granting of a license to individuals or groups to perform specific commercial activities. The franchisor and franchisee form a relationship that benefits both parties through expansion of the brand and local operation. The activities of a franchise vary from business to business and depend upon the type of product or service involved.

Even with this base knowledge, franchises can be confusing. Often people are confused by the various types of franchises, the terms used, and the differences between a license and a franchise and how a franchise works.

There are four common types of franchises: business format franchises, product distribution franchises, film and media franchises, and sports franchises. Following is a brief description of each type of franchise.

Business Format Franchises

The most common type of franchise is the business format franchise. According to the IFA (International Franchise Association), of the more than 800,000 franchises in the United States in 2016, 88% of them were business format franchises.[5]

A business format franchise grants the franchisee a license. The license gives the franchise the following benefits:

- The right to sell the franchisor's service or product

- The right to use their trademark and brand name

- The operation manuals, systems, and processes to conduct business

The franchisor benefits by:

- Business expansion with less capital outlay

- Receiving ongoing royalty payments

- Opening more units, which equals higher brand recognition and more royalties

The franchise agreement varies significantly by the franchise, the type of business, and the length of time the franchise has been in business. The most common business format franchises are restaurants (quick service and table), lodging, business services (examples: printers, signs, insurance, financial services) and personal services (hair salons, healthcare, spa). These typically require a storefront and a higher level of investment than other types of franchises. Business format franchises also include mobile services and consumer services. Examples are travel planning, janitorial, lawn care, home maintenance, and business consulting.

Almost nine out of ten franchises are set up as a business format concept. The franchisee is paying for the rights to use the franchisor's structures, brand, training, and support in exchange for a license to do business using their methods. The business is usually tied to a specific territory and performs according to the specifications outlined in the franchise agreement.

Product Distribution Franchising

The second type of franchise is the product distribution franchise. These franchises are supplier-dealer relationships. A product distribution franchise obtains a license to distribute a product or supply a service to others. The critical difference between a product distribution and a business format franchise is that the franchisor does not usually provide an entire system to run the business. One of the first product distribution franchises was the Coca-Cola Company, which allowed individuals to bottle and distribute the product all over the U.S.

The most common types of product distribution franchises are automotive/truck dealers, beverages, food, and gasoline stations. Many other product distribution franchises operate on a smaller scale. Other examples of product distribution franchises are companies that distribute tires, lawn tractors, paint, and vending. This type of business may qualify as a business opportunity since the company does not have the same control over the distribution franchise as a business format franchise. The amount of control varies by the license agreement.

Film or Media Franchise

Often I talk with individuals who are confused about movie franchises. A series of films or movies are known as film or media franchises. Harry Potter, Star Wars, and Batman are all film/movie franchises. The film companies grant the theaters the rights to show the movie or broadcast it on television. Rights are granted through licensing agreements. A good example is the Harry Potter Series by J. K. Rowling. In her *Be your own Harry Potter* blog, Cherie Oswald explains how J. K. Rowling licensed the Harry Potter book series to Warner Brothers Studios. In J. K. Rowling's original negotiation in 1999, the studio received movie, merchandise, and other rights to the stories. Rowling had the foresight to hold on to the rights to the characters. Because Warner was restricted to the stories themselves, they were permitted to change the stories or create new stories.

Oswald says, "Because it was such a large franchise, and the brand had so many possible applications, Warner sublicensed to toy manufacturers like Hasbro and Mattel, candy manufacturers like Jelly Belly, and theme park builders like Universal Studios. Between movies and merchandise alone, Harry Potter has racked up over $15 billion in sales."[6]

Technically, any movie that is licensed is a franchise. However, most people refer to a series of movies when they talk about a "film franchise."

Media franchises include copyrighted works such as books, magazines, musical recordings, and video games. These licenses are granted for the use of the media and characters in other products, such as toys, games, books, and posters.

Sports Franchise

The Oxford University Press defines a sports franchise as an ownership structure in professional sports in which a league is limited to a fixed number of teams.[7] The owners of a team are granted territorial rights to avoid competition in an area. The National Football League (NFL) and the National Basketball Association (NBA) are two well-known sports leagues in the United States. Each team in the league is licensed as a franchise. Licensing agreements give distributors the right to manufacture and sell products associated with the team.

For the purposes of this book, we will focus on business format franchises because they are the most common types and the most accessible for the general public.

Table 1.1 The State of Franchising in the United States

According to data in "The Economic Impact of Franchised Businesses: Volume IV, 2016," in 2016:

- There were 801,153 franchised businesses.

- Franchised businesses provided 8,968,000 jobs or 5.6 percent of the U.S. private non-farm workforce.

- Franchised businesses supplied an annual payroll of $351.1 billion, or 3.8 percent of all private non-farm payrolls.

- Franchised business produced goods and services worth $868.1 billion, or 2.8 percent of private non-farm output.

- Gross Domestic Product (GDP) of franchise businesses totaled $541.1 billion, or 3.4 percent of all private non-farm GDP.[8]

- There are an estimated 3,000 different franchisors (franchise business companies) in the U.S.

These statistics demonstrate the significant impact franchising has on our national economy.

FRANCHISE MYTHS

As with any business, many myths about franchises keep individuals from moving forward. Just like the "grapevine game" we played as children, information is passed and as it passes from one person to another it changes and becomes something entirely different from the facts. These falsehoods block potential business owners and franchisees from their dreams. Do not fall into the trap of believing these myths about franchising.

Myth 1: I will need to have experience in the business before buying a franchise.

Not true. The majority of franchises do not require you to have experience in the industry you are considering. There are specific skill sets that work when running a business consistent with all categories of business. The methods franchises have in place are designed to help you be successful without direct experience in the industry. Franchisors desire someone who can manage others and support their proven systems. Look at your transferable skills and hire people to fill in the skills you lack.

Often, people appeal to the myth that they do not have the experience necessary as a reason to stay in their comfort zone. Moving out of your comfort zone is a chance to learn and grow and through buying a franchise your discomfort can be lessened.

Myth 2: I need to find a business in a field where I am passionate.

There is a difference between passion and motivation. Sometimes people start a business based on their hobby, favorite sport, or pastime. Be careful: you may end up hating the hobby if you are trying to make money out of it.

Do not be afraid to explore options that never occurred to you. Conducting a thorough, systematic search for a franchise based on your goals may open up new passions and possibilities.

Keep in mind, too, that the chances for success will be higher when you are motivated. One person's passion is another person's folly. That is the beauty of our humanity—we all have different skill sets, motivations, and desires.

Myth 3: Buying a "hot franchise" is best

Sometimes a new brand comes in and becomes a "hot" market item, and everyone wants to get in on the trend. Or people will ask me, "What's the hottest franchise right now?" Do not fall for the allure of buying the "hottest new brand" of franchise.

Newer franchises are known as "emerging brands." These franchises have only been opened a short period and have 10 or fewer units in place. These more unique brands add risk, and their growth spurt usually slows after a while. Once the trend has died down, will you still like what you are doing? Take into account the day-to-day activities of running the business and the potential for success down the road.

Occasionally I run into someone who says that they bought into a trendy franchise a few years ago and it was a big mistake. They lost time and money in the endeavor and wished they had not taken the chance they did. Jim Judy, a Consultant at FranChoice, says, "Selecting a franchise business to grow as your own should not be a gamble. You are not making a quick bet on a favored horse or a booming stock. [You] are making a major investment in a new life that will impact [yourself, your family,] and possibly future generations, for decades."[9]

While some people are well-suited to an emerging brand, be sure to evaluate these options carefully. The answer to the question, "Which franchise is hot right now?" is "the one that is right for *you*." Don't get caught up in the promise of a quick buck. Focus instead on your business skills, interests, personal aspirations, and your budget.

Myth 4: Every franchise is successful

Unfortunately, every business has the potential to fail. Even if you have a model to follow. It's up to the owner (YOU!) to follow the directions and work hard for the business to succeed. The groundwork is in place to help you achieve; be sure to adhere to the foundation and be consistent. There are no perfect models. Look for a brand that is working on continuous improvement and offers support to their franchisees so everyone is successful.

Myth 5: It's easy to make money because a franchise is an out-of-the-box business

Marcus Lemonis, the host of TV's *The Profit*, spoke at the IFA convention in 2016, and when asked about misconceptions of owning a franchise, he stated, "I think often people buy a franchise, and they sometimes think that you're going to get this business in a box and everything is going to turn out."[10] In other words, it's not about easy. While it is often true that things will "turn out" if you follow the system, you should plan to use extra elbow grease to see your efforts come to fruition.

Lemonis went on to say passion must drive you more than making a lot of money: "Some people get into the business because they think it is a get rich quick scheme, or they think it is the next big hit and they do not want to miss out. And what I prefer is that people got involved in things they believe in."[11]

We have covered five myths about franchising. Now we focus on the pros and cons of owning a franchise.

PROS AND CONS OF FRANCHISING

While there are many reasons for someone to choose franchising as a business model. It is essential to clarify general advantages and disadvantages of purchasing a franchise. Knowledge of the potential gains and losses will contribute to choosing good opportunities.

Pros

Brand. The brand of a company is an easily recognizable marketing tool, logo, and verbal and visual identity that customers use to recognize a business. The brand is used for all marketing communications. As a franchise, the brand should be in place and recognizable. A brand is one of the most significant benefits of owning a franchise. Your business will ramp up faster and go farther with a brand name. The brand is what brings in customers that may not patronize an independent business of the same type.

Marketing. Marketing and advertising for your franchise business have already been developed and tested. The franchise can pool the resources of all franchises to create quality campaigns and professional advertisements. Keeping up with marketing and advertising is daunting and very expensive for an independent business; therefore, marketing is a significant advantage.

Proven Systems. Routines and procedures for effective operation are in place, along with training manuals and replicable processes. These methods have been tried and tested. Brad Sugars, founder of ActionCOACH says, "One of the best things about buying into a franchise opportunity is that you don't have to reinvent the wheel to be successful."[12]

Faster start-up. Through the purchase of a franchised business, challenges to a start-up are significantly reduced. The franchise has opened multiple units; therefore, they have a great deal of experience with the grand opening and start-up. They should have developed processes that will assist in getting the business off to a good start.

Financial Assistance. Franchises have a good track record of success. Therefore, banks are more likely to loan to potential franchisees than independent business start-ups. Besides, several financial partners work with the franchises to assist in financing and alternative methods of making the investment.

Management. The principal management of a franchise system often has many years of experience running franchises. This experience is valuable to franchisees both in having a guide to opening their business and in having a model for managing their own employees.

Technology. As technology advances, the franchise's software and equipment will require regular updates to stay secure or to improve processes. In a franchise, the cost to update is shared across franchisees, making it more economical than for an independent business.

Defined Territory. Depending on the franchise, there can be assigned areas. Defined regions are an advantage because they keep other franchises of the same brand from infringing upon your customers. Having a defined territory makes it easier to market within your assigned area.

A built-in network. When you open a franchise, you are not alone as a business owner. You have the development team of the franchise and other franchisees to turn to for support and advice. This team advantage is valuable as you have someone to turn to who has been there before and can share best practices. With the support and training of a franchisor, you will always have someone to assist you in your business.

Consistency. Uniformity in food, products, and services is one significant advantage of franchise operations. When visiting a franchise, customers already expect to find a particular quality of product or service because of the brand name reputation. If you visit a franchised tire shop in Ohio versus the same brand in Colorado, you expect the same service and quality of tires. When you eat at a franchised restaurant, you expect the same food quality and service no matter where it is located.

Cons

Limits on your Independence. A franchisee is required to follow the methods and procedures outlined in the franchise agreement. While you may be able to challenge things, doing so in the wrong way or too often will probably be frowned upon by the franchisor and could result in a loss of the franchise license.

Royalties. Royalties are fees paid by the franchisee for the use of the licensing, trademarks, and methods outlined in the franchise agreement. These are typically paid based on gross sales but sometimes are based on a flat fee or product purchases. Royalties go to the franchisor and allow them to continue their support and to improve and promote the brand. Royalties are typically taken out of gross sales and they do affect your income.

Territory Restrictions. There may be times when you receive requests to service customers outside of your defined territory boundaries, but as a franchisee you will be unable to meet those customers' needs. At best, you might be able to refer them to the franchisee local to the customer.

Capital Outlay. There is more capital needed in the beginning to open a franchise due to the franchise investment fee. This investment up front with the franchise gives you the rights to use their licenses, trademarks, branding, and systems in your business. While that investment may feel steep at the time, those initial franchise costs are generally offset by the support, training, and faster start of the franchise model versus independent business model.

Agreement Time Frame. A franchise agreement is for a specified period of years—often ten years, sometimes five years, or even twenty years. At the end of the contract, a franchisee with good status typically has the option to renew their agreement. The time frame can be a disadvantage if the franchisee wants to leave the business before the end of the contract. If the franchisee cannot sell the business, they will need to pay additional fees. Additional fees or a lump sum are spelled out in the agreement.

These pros and cons are far from inclusive of all franchises. Each franchise model will have it is own variations since they are all different. For a genuine franchise contender, the above list is a useful starting checklist of items to consider when looking at individual franchises.

WORKING WITH FRANCHISE CONSULTANTS

When making the life-changing decision of purchasing a franchise, it is essential to obtain advice from professionals before making a final decision.

One of the first professionals you should consult with is a franchise consultant; they have the knowledge to help you make an informed decision. Similar to a realtor that assists in finding a home for your family, a franchise consultant assists in finding a franchise that suits you. Most franchise consultants are registered through various organizations such as BAI (Business Alliance, Inc.), FranNet, FranChoice, IFPG, or Entrepreneur's Source. They have gone through wide-ranging training programs in all areas of the industry and often have franchise experience. These professionals spend countless hours studying the industry, getting to know the franchisors, and keeping abreast of current trends. Utilizing this knowledge can prove invaluable.

Working with a franchise consultant, also known as a franchise coach, advisor, specialist or broker, will provide you with priceless insight into your business search. Not only will they help you limit your choices to a good fit, you will also save time, money, and aggravation. Their proven methodical processes will help you choose the franchise that is right for you.

Benefits of Working with a Franchise Advisor

Narrows your choices. Your franchise coach will help you create a personal profile and narrow your options to businesses that will meet your goals and aspirations. Besides, they will check for territory availability before presenting you with options. Why waste time researching franchises that are not available to you? A franchise consultant will make sure your time and energy are spent on the opportunities that are worthwhile to you.

Insider knowledge of franchises. A franchise consultant knows about franchisors' validation process, systems, support, training, and more. They are some of the first people to know about new, emerging brands. Although some of this information is protected and not to be disclosed, they can help steer you in the right direction.

Franchise consultations are typically at no cost. Most franchise consultation services cost you nothing. Franchise consultants are retained by the franchise companies to present candidates who possess the qualifications necessary to be successful. The consultant is typically paid on commission, similar to a realtor, and they will want you to find a business that works for you.

Knowledgeable about funding options. Franchise consultants know about the various funding options and can assist you with resources of funding for your franchise. Resources include 401K rollovers and SBA guaranteed loans.

Connections with the right people. During your consultation, you will be introduced to the franchisor that can make your dreams a reality. While making these business introductions on an individual level may be a challenge, with a consultant's help, building this business relationship with a high-level franchisor is much easier.

Eliminate the guesswork and save yourself time and frustration by working with a professional franchise consultant. They will take an unbiased look at your interests and create a detailed profile based on your preferences. Also, they will provide a great deal of information and guidance through the franchise investigation process. Working with a franchise consultant will give you alternatives you may not have considered, giving you more chances to make the right choice.

SURPRISING FACTS ABOUT FRANCHISING

Franchising is a great way to own a business that provides proven systems, marketing, training, and support. If you are beginning your search for the right franchise, you may find the following facts about franchising surprising.

The sheer number of franchises

No one knows how many individual franchise concepts exist since it is a number that is continually changing. There are anywhere from 3,000 to 5,000 different franchise concepts, with more emerging every day.

Buying a franchise is not easy

Each franchise has a process with a certain number of steps to follow to determine if the franchise is a good fit. This process can be involved and generally requires that you as the potential franchisee follow a series of steps. After all, the franchisor wants to work with franchisees that will support their methods and procedures; if the prospective franchisee will not follow the steps to determine if the franchise is right for them, that's a sign they may not be the right prospect.

Anyone can franchise his or her business

Anyone who feels their business is viable for franchising, wants to go through the legal qualifications, and has the capital, can set up a franchise. Beware, therefore, of emerging franchises, especially if the owners do not have franchise experience.

The franchise fee is not the only cost to own a franchise

Other expenses depend on the franchise type, location, training, inventories, royalties, and other requirements. Be sure to check the Franchise Disclosure Document (FDD) for the list of expected expenses.

The franchise provides the tools, the franchisee does the work

Every franchisee is in control of their own destiny
—Marcus Lemonis

The franchise provides the training, tools, and instructions on how to start and run your business. Their playbook is for you to read, digest, and follow. It is up to you as the owner to run the business, attract customers, and keep customers. You (again, *the owner*) must do the day-to-day work, and that is challenging even when you buy a franchise. The franchise makes it easier, but you will need to be able to follow their instructions and procedures to be successful.

Marcus Lemonis emphasizes that it takes a lot of work and staying connected to the business for it to thrive. He sees many stories of success when people buy average franchise concepts and put in extra effort and realize positive results. Take advantage of the benefits of the franchise, don't expect them to do the work, add extra effort, and plan to flourish.

Franchising is a profitable and popular opportunity

Even with fees, legal concerns, and lengthy application procedures, franchising remains a popular and profitable opportunity, and the franchise industry is growing every day in numbers of franchisors, units, employees, and franchisees.

Now that you have more knowledge about what franchising is, hopefully some of your fear has lessened. In the next section we are going to help you dive into whether you *should* go into business. This section will help you prepare for confronting the fear that is holding you back from making a change.

START A BUSINESS OR BUY A FRANCHISE?

One of the central questions people ask is, "Should I start a business or buy a franchise?" This section will help you answer this question with information on different pathways to owning a business and factors leading to success for various types of ownership. In addition, we will look at the many categories of franchised businesses to provide you with insight into the wide variety available. First, we will go over motives people have for going into business.

Reasons to Go into Business

Often you hear the thousands of reasons not to go into business. In fact, there are lots of reasons *to go* into business.

Flexibility. In the beginning, you'll work more extended hours for less pay, and this pays off when over time, you will be able to set your hours. You *will* need to work long hours. However, you can work whenever it suits your schedule. Stay up late or get up early, you choose. While on the one hand, if you do not work, you do not get paid, on the other hand, if you enjoy what you are doing, it won't seem like work.

I recently read an article about a woman who was working corporate and had a small son. She wanted to stay at home with her son, so she began a cleaning business on the side. Now she is CEO of a large corporate cleaning business and never misses a ball game or activity. She sets her hours around his schedule. Her husband now has a role in the company too.

Tax benefits. When you own a business, you can take advantage of tax deductions. You can write off expenses for your business such as travel, home office, food, phone bills, and so on. There are even some government incentives for starting a business. Be sure to research your options. Check with an accountant for eligible tax expenses.

Pass down to future generations. When you own your own business, you have something you can pass on to the next generation. A family business is something to be proud of because you created it. Many franchisees are passing their franchise on to the next generation as well. Building a business where your sons and daughters can work and carry on your success is very satisfying.

Job security. If you have ever been laid off, downsized, underemployed, or fired, you know how illusory a "steady job" is. When you own your own business, you are your own boss. You won't have to worry about someone else determining your future.

Giving back. When owning a business, you have the option of giving back to the community. Since you control where your money goes, you can sponsor a charity, a non-profit, or other community activity. It's a good feeling to be able to give to others. You will also have the opportunity to improve the environment by making environmentally conscious choices.

Freshness. When you own a business, you wear many hats, especially, in the beginning. Every day will present new experiences and challenges. The newness provides owners with a fresh perspective and learning experiences. There is always room for improvement, and you will have the upper hand when it comes to making those decisions.

Develop Skills. Mike Templeman, CEO of Foxtail Marketing, says, "People ask me how I learned about SEO, social media, pay-per-click, PR, and all the other marketing techniques I utilize. I tell them that I was forced to learn them, otherwise I wouldn't survive. While developing new skills can be tough and takes time, it can pay off in spades. These skills will be invaluable throughout your life."[13]

The skills I have picked up through owning my own businesses are varied, valuable, and beneficial. I often say it's enough for a Ph.D. in business!

Become an expert. If you stick with your business long enough, you will soon become known as an expert. Once known as an expert, you will develop other skills through marketing, writing, and even speaking about your business.

Acknowledgment. There are many opportunities for recognition for business owners. You can be recognized at the local, regional, and national level in every field and industry. Our local business newspaper, *Columbus Business First*[14], seems to announce a new awards banquet every month. You'll feel incredible satisfaction if you are recognized for your success in this way.

Financial independence. Most people go into business for financial independence. How do you define financial independence? Do you want to retire wealthy, make more money than you are now, or have the money to buy what you want? Owning a business does not guarantee financial independence, but it can allow you to achieve it. People say, "You get out of it what you put into it"—this is very true for business.

Reinvention. Mike Templeman gives an excellent example of the opportunity for reinvention: "I've started and sold several companies over my career. And every time I sell a company, I'm presented with an opportunity to reinvent myself all over again. On the flip side, if I had received my law degree, I'd be a lawyer (not a lot of room to recreate myself). However, as an entrepreneur, I get to be whatever I want to be."[15]

I feel the same way. I have owned a retail gift shop, a wholesale business, a horse-riding and training business, a franchising consulting business, and now a fundraising franchise. With each new endeavor, I learn new ways of doing business. The education and knowledge I obtain are precious to me. Knowledge is power and owning a business is powerful.

Change the world. Many people have changed the world with their companies. They all started somewhere. Apple started in a garage. Bill Gates started from very little. You may be one who will change the world. It's a good thought. It is possible.

Control over whom you work with. One of the most frustrating aspects of working in a corporate environment is the lack of control over with whom you work. As a business owner, you get to choose your employees. Working with people who fit your culture and personality makes your day much more pleasant. If they do not work out, well, you know, you can show them the door.

You also have control over your customers. If they give you too many headaches, you can show them the door, too.

Your why

Why do you want to own a business? What drives you? Most people want to control their destiny, be their boss, build equity, and obtain more flexibility. One of the most common reasons I hear is, "I want to work hard for myself, not someone else." Some people want to help their community, have financial independence, or be creative. Of course, the most important reason is the one that gets you to quit that corporate job and finally go into business for yourself!

COGNITIVE OVERLOAD

Making decisions is difficult because of the many options that are available to us. There is research available to help us make effective decisions.

In *Simplicity: The New Competitive Advantage*, Bill Jensen presents research on how people make decisions based on a survey of over 2,500 people. He found a pattern of five questions that, when people could answer them, led to action:

1. How is this [decision] relevant to what I do?

2. What, precisely should I do?

3. How will I be measured, and what are the consequences?

4. What tools and support are available?

5. WIIFM—What's In It For Me? For us?[16]

Jensen's research suggested the question about tools and resources was the most important. He attributes this to the *cognitive overload* we're all experiencing from the overwhelming amount of information available everywhere.

Throughout this book, I present you with tools you can use to help you avoid cognitive overload and make effective decisions.

Information is the resolution of uncertainty.
—Claude Shannon

THREE PATHWAYS FOR OWNING A BUSINESS

There are several pathways to owning a business. The three most traveled paths are:

1. Start an independent business from scratch and go it alone.

2. Purchase a franchise and be in business for yourself, not by yourself.

3. Purchase an existing business.

There are advantages and disadvantages for each option. The ideal pathway for you depends upon your situation, goals, interests, timing, and financial capabilities. First, let's start with considerations to bear in mind when starting an independent business.

Independent business

The simplest type of business to understand is the independent business or sole-proprietorship. An independent business is started from scratch. Through research and exploration, an individual or group of people determine a product or service to sell, write a business plan, develop marketing and advertising, oversee and perform the day-to-day operations of the business, and are solely responsible for the financing. The owner of an independent business has full control over all operations of the business.

Factors leading to success when you start a business from scratch

1. A product or service that has enough potential customers to turn a profit in a reasonable period.

2. Time to plan for all aspects of the business.

3. A careful, well-planned start-up phase.

4. The skillful acquisition of new and lasting customers.

5. Ample capital to invest in test marketing and advertising.

6. Ability to hire efficient employees.

7. Effective training programs for employees.

8. Finding the right location demographically and geographically.

9. Professional advisors or mentors to call on for assistance as needed.

10. Realizing that you are alone—all decisions will be up to you to make.

Starting your own business is a dream for countless people. If you are the independent type who is a self-starter, have an excellent business plan, and are willing to take the risk to start from scratch, you may well be very successful. However, if you want less risk, feel more comfortable with a proven business, and desire the assistance of experienced professionals, then a franchise might provide the answer.

Franchised business

Franchises give hundreds of thousands of Americans and individuals around the globe the chance to own a business. Through franchising, individuals and families have the opportunity to start a business with the expertise of a franchise. They are in business "for themselves, but not by themselves." Franchisees grow the business, offer employment to people in their community, and provide for their family. In addition, their business will improve the local economy through purchases of inventory and services from other businesses in the community.

Franchises allow people to build equity during the time they are in business. By building equity, they can later sell the business or pass it on to their children. There are thousands of family-owned franchises that are passing their trade down to the next generation. Every day several people sign franchise agreements and many more renew their contracts for another term. Plumbers, cleaners, printers, and handymen are switching their companies over to franchises to reap the rewards of proven systems, a well-known brand name, technological advances, and marketing expertise.

If not for franchising, these opportunities would not be available to individuals desiring to own a business without starting from scratch. Through the purchase of a franchised business, challenges to a start-up are significantly reduced, and the potential to build a business into a profitable enterprise is impressive.

Factors to success for a franchised business compared to an independent business

1. Proven product or service already in place.

2. Faster start-up because of the systems in place and assistance you will receive.

3. Easier preparation of a business plan.

4. Marketing and advertising have been tested and proven.

5. Easier, faster customer acquisition because the already established brand promotes trust with customers.

6. More access to funding than with an independent start-up.

7. In many cases, franchisor assistance with employee training or materials to help you train the people you hire.

8. Help finding the ideal location—franchisors have guidelines in place and often will assist in helping you find a great location.

9. Access to the franchisor for advice and assistance if you are not sure what to do about an issue. Other franchisees often offer valuable information.

10. In most cases, technology updates from the franchisor that an independent business might struggle to afford.

Even though you are buying a franchise, you will still want to write a formal business plan. The business plan will help you clarify your goals, plan for your finances, and strategize your business. Not to mention if you are looking to finance your business, the bank will require a formal business plan.

Each franchise provides various benefits, training, and support. Be sure to understand the features and benefits of the businesses you are considering.

One point to make here, when you are deciding between starting a business from scratch and purchasing a franchise, there is less to worry about with a franchise. There is so much information to be gleaned from actual franchisees and the franchise company itself, and this knowledge makes your decision much more comfortable than going it alone starting a business from scratch. There are many more unknowns when starting a business from nothing.

Buying an existing business

For those who are risk-adverse, need cash flow immediately, and have the capital, an existing business or resale franchise might be the answer. Compared to buying a start-up franchise and setting up a store from scratch, when you buy an established business or resale franchise, the business already exists in some form. The location is set, and your business is up and running when you walk in the door.

Let's examine factors to contemplate when buying an existing business or resale franchise.

1. Thoroughly check out the financials of the business before purchasing. Be sure to have a qualified accountant or work with a business broker to assist with this task. The advantage here is that you have records and history of financials to project potential revenues.

2. The investment in a resale business is much higher than for a startup. An existing business may cost 2–5 times the cost of starting from scratch.

3. There is no lag time between the preparation and start-up phase and time to cash flow. You will be in business right away when purchasing a resale business. Hopefully, the business is already in positive cash flow.

4. If there are problems with the business, you may not find out until after you buy the enterprise.

5. Trained employees that stay with the new owner can be quite an advantage when buying a business because they can keep the shop running while you're still learning the ropes.

6. Employees who remain with the company can also be a disadvantage insofar as they are not people you have chosen. There is a chance for personality conflicts.

7. Check the lease thoroughly. The business may be bound to a contract for an extended period, or the location may not be ideal.

8. Be aware of any old or outdated processes, equipment, inventory, or technology that may need expensive updates or repairs.

9. When buying what someone else has built, you do not have the opportunity to put your stamp on the business.

10. There is a chance of losing customers, as they may not like the change in ownership. On the other hand, you will have an excellent opportunity to reinvent the business and make it even better than with the past owner.

11. Buying a well-established business can be quite an advantage if you do not want to start from nothing and need cash flow immediately.

The answer to the question, "Should I buy an existing business, start-up my own business, or buy a franchise?" is—*It depends*. It depends on your goals, interests, financial state, timing, skills, and many other factors. There are advantages and disadvantages to each option. Carefully think through the options, ask for professional advice and conduct a solid investigation before making your final decision to make your dream a reality.

BUSINESS OPPORTUNITIES VERSUS FRANCHISED BUSINESSES

Sometimes people ask, "What is the difference between an independent business, a business opportunity, and a franchised business?" Untangling these terms and uses of these business options is actually pretty easy.

What is a Business Opportunity?

A business opportunity has several definitions, and the legal requirements vary from state to state. The Federal Trade Commission (FTC) regulates business opportunities, and some states impose additional regulations. For our purposes, *a business opportunity is a packaged business investment that allows the buyer to begin a business.*

If you're thinking, "But doesn't that mean a franchise is a business opportunity?" you're right—it is. However, it's only *one kind* of business opportunity; not all business opportunities are franchises. The most significant difference is in the Federal Trade Commission

(FTC) requirements for a business opportunity and a franchise. The FTC has strict rules for franchises and requires a Franchise Disclosure Document (FDD) be prepared and approved by the FTC before the business can operate as a franchise. You may want to check out their website at https://ftc.gov.

With a business opportunity, you usually pay a fee for the opportunity to begin a business selling products or services. The company often provides equipment, training, website access, and materials to help you sell. Many business opportunities are home-based. One noteworthy difference is that a franchisor exercises more control over the franchisees than a business opportunity.

Most business opportunities do not charge a royalty fee, however typically charge a percentage of the products purchased or require that product be bought through the parent company. It is often an advantage to purchase products through the parent company as they buy in bulk and can pass the savings on to the owner. With a business opportunity, the owner typically does not own the right to license the trade name however they can give their business a different name. Several states have licensing requirements for business opportunities.

Some examples of business opportunities are Tupperware, Mary Kay, Amway, and Legal Shield (These are also known as multi-level marketing companies or MLM's). There are other business opportunities in home health care, employment, and vending, and these require a more substantial investment. A business opportunity allows more freedom than a franchise but fewer legal protections and less support. Product distribution franchises are often classified as business opportunities. Be sure to find out if you are looking at a business opportunity or a franchise.

See the table below for a brief comparison of business options.

Table 1. Comparison of Types of Business*

	FRANCHISE	BUSINESS OPPORTUNITY	START-UP BUSINESS	BUY EXISTING BUSINESS	BUY EXISTING FRANCHISE
BRANDING	Branding in place and established	Some branding may be in place	Must build the brand from scratch	Established business	Established business
DISCLOSURE DOCUMENT	FDD– Franchise Disclosure Document (FTC requirement)	No FDD requirement. Some states have rules that must be followed	No FDD	No FDD if not a franchise	FDD
SUPPORT	Support Of franchisor	Support varies	No support	Support from existing owner possible	Support from franchisor
SYSTEMS	Proven systems in place	Varies	No established systems	Varies	Proven systems in place
TRAINING	Training by franchisor	Some training	Entrepreneur responsible for his or her own training	Training by owner or employees	Training by franchisor and owner
FRANCHISE FEE	Franchise fee	Fee for start-up equipment	No external fees	No	Franchisee fee or transfer fee
ROYALTIES	Royalties paid to franchisor	Costs vary, but usually not an ongoing royalty fee	No royalties	No royalties	Royalties paid to franchisor

*All information varies between businesses, type of business, company, product, and service.

CATEGORIES OF FRANCHISE BUSINESS

Food is by far not the only franchise option!

We usually think of fast-food chains when we think of franchises. However, there are franchises in many different industries—over 70 different categories exist. For this reason, it is challenging to determine the business and franchise options that would be a good fit for your goals. With dozens of categories of franchises ranging from A to Z, it is easy to get caught up in the options. There is even a category of "miscellaneous and unique" franchise options. Be sure to check out the list of common franchise categories in Table 2 and highlight ones that seem most interesting.

When considering a franchise, you will want to scrutinize the differences between franchises in a category. It is easier to narrow your options to a few types and then look at one or two concepts in a group, rather than looking at too many options and risk *cognitive overload*.

Table 2. Common categories of franchised businesses

- Advertising & Marketing
- Automotive
- Beverages
- Building & Storage
- Business Services
- Children's Services
- Computer/Technology
- Convenience Stores
- Dry Cleaning & Laundry
- Employment & Personnel
- Education
- Financial
- Food
- Hair Styling
- Health & Fitness
- Home Based
- Ice Cream & Yogurt

- Lawn & Garden
- Maid Service & Janitorial
- Maintenance
- Management & Training
- Miscellaneous & Unique
- Packaging & Mailing
- Pet Care
- Printing/Photocopying & Signs
- Real Estate
- Repair and Restoration
- Retail
- Security Services
- Senior Care
- Sports
- Tanning
- Travel & Tourism
- Vending

Low-cost franchises

Many individuals open businesses because they would like to have more flexibility with their time. Businesses that are franchised and offer a lower-investment appeal to many career changers due to less financial risk involved. The lower investment is a factor because the business can be run from home or a lower-rent location without the expensive build-out other franchises require. These franchises are often home-based, less complicated to operate, and sometimes comprise a mobile service. Services are by appointment or contract rather than walk-ins or storefront, giving the owner much more flexibility with their schedule. Some people call these *job franchises* because it may give the impression the owner is buying him/herself a job.

WHAT THE FRANCHISOR WANTS

We could say "myth 6" is that the franchisor just wants to sell more units. In fact, the franchisor wants much more than that, and it's helpful to have an idea of what a franchisor is looking for so you can determine if you have the kind of make-up to succeed in a franchise model.

First and foremost, the franchise business *wants you to succeed*. When franchisees are thriving, the brand thrives, too, and thus the franchisor thrives. That also means when one party suffers, the other does, too, and that, of course, can lead to friction. You sink or swim together. It is essential that both parties are comfortable with the arrangement and feel they work together well for both the good times and the bad.

Roles or Backgrounds

Franchisors are looking for franchisees who fit a specific profile. No one skill set means inevitable success or failure, however, a handful of work experiences give franchisees a leg up.

The franchisor often seeks out individuals who have experience in sales or marketing. The owner needs to be able to bring in customers, and without sales skills or the willingness to learn sales, it may not be a good fit. The sales requirements depend upon the franchise, so be sure to ask how much and what kind of selling will be needed. Moreover, experiences in certain roles can indicate to a franchisor that you will be capable of running a successful business.

Sales Professionals. Individuals with sales skills and capabilities make naturally great franchise candidates. As we have discussed earlier, people who have worked in sales are usually high potential franchisees. They are driven to succeed by increasing sales and enjoy talking to customers and working with people.

Accountants. Accountants understand the finances of the organization and have a solid background in business management. They are typically detail-oriented and often excel at running their own business or franchise. Accountants understand the various departments of a company and often have familiarity working with teams.

Managers. Management experience and the ability to manage people are excellent skills for running a business. Managers have various abilities depending on their experiences. These skills can transfer to business owners because of their involvements with human resources, retail management, office management, financial operations, and plant or operations management. People who have excellent leadership skills excel at running a franchise.

Keep in mind that a great manager can adapt to management in most businesses; it is about managing people and operations. Therefore, if you are an experienced manager, your options are quite open, and you may want to explore areas that you are less familiar with to expand your possibilities.

Health and medical franchises seek individuals who have experience managing people, a medical sales or nursing background, and enjoy working with people. A confident personality is a must in this profession. Often, people come into the home health industry because of past involvements with a loved one or skills in the healthcare industry.

Restaurant franchises. There are food franchises that only accept franchisees who have experience running a restaurant. The franchisors past practices have demonstrated to them that people with restaurant experience are the most successful for their brand. Restaurant know-how is not always a prerequisite—be sure to check with the franchise for their requirements.

Sports Professionals

Some sports professionals purchase franchises and start their businesses after time in the major leagues. Professional athletes make great franchisees and franchisors due to their athletic training to be disciplined, motivated, and follow a playbook.

Nancy Williams writes about Barry Word and his franchise. Barry Word played NFL football with the Kansas City Chiefs from 1990 to 1992. He owns a SpeedPro Imaging Franchise, which creates large-format graphics for businesses. Word likes the fact that franchising comes with a "playbook" to follow and as an athlete he can easily relate to following playbooks. SpeedPro franchisees work together for the benefit of their businesses, and this teamwork is another benefit of owning a franchise—you have people to turn to when you have a question or problem. You also have people with whom to share opportunities and achievements.

Word says, "Professional athletes should determine how they want to spend the rest of their lives while they're still playing."[17]

From athlete to franchisor

Tafa Jefferson is known for being one of the first professional athletes to start a franchise. Jefferson is a former offensive lineman for the Chicago Bears and founded the franchise Amada Senior Care in 2013. I interviewed Tafa in December, 2018 about his experiences in franchising and how the skills learned as an athlete transferred to business.

How did you get into franchising?

Tafa: I started with a home care business and did not consider becoming a franchisor until someone mentioned that the best way to expand would be to franchise. This conversation caused me to contemplate franchising and once I understood the power of the model I got behind it. Amada Senior Care started franchising in 2013 and has grown exponentially to 120+ locations throughout the U.S.

Tafa enjoys the way franchising has grown the business, presents entrepreneurs the opportunity to own a business, gives employees meaningful work, and provides a valuable service to seniors and their families. The franchise model has allowed us to grow our brand and expanded our ability to serve more seniors in a tremendous way.

Tafa has used skills he learned during his time in the NFL and in business school to grow his franchise. His passion for entrepreneurship and caring for others fits well with his senior care business.

How do your experiences as an athlete relate to business ownership and becoming a franchisor?

Tafa: Participation in athletics provides a great foundation for starting a business. Collegiate and professional athletic career skills transfer to business quickly. Those transferable skills sets, include—preparation, practical application through studies, managing time while maintaining a full-time course load responsibility. As an athlete, you keep your fitness top of mind, you prepare with training, proper diet, and need to be mentally strong. The same attributes cross-over into business. I refer to it as a corporate athlete.

Are there other traits that transfer from athletes to business?

Tafa: Additional traits that are equally important for both athletes and running a business successfully are—personality, dedication, and discipline. Mentoring is another aspect that relates to both athletes and business. While an athlete coaches others to take on important skill sets, a franchisor supports new franchisees through the many aspects and challenges of starting the business, growing the business, and maintaining the business.

What is more, ability to find resources are important in order to start a business, one must be able to secure the necessary resources—same as an athlete. Tafa has found that people who are not successful and fall short, may not have planned appropriately, or may not have secured proper resources to make it through the challenging aspects of starting the business.

According to Tafa, one of the benefits of starting a business is, if you are successful in one business venture, you will find that starting new ventures are easier because you know what to expect. The process can be replicated with different products, services, and various industries. He also considers his failures as valuable lessons he has used to learn what to do and what not to do.

What differentiates Amada Senior Care from other franchises in this space?

Tafa: While there are many senior care franchises, Amada Senior Care differentiates itself by taking a holistic approach for their clients, offering a variety of services. Amada specializes in assisting families through the Long Term Care Insurance claims process. They value their franchisees and have a franchisee first mentality.

How have you seen fear affect people looking to buy a franchise?

Tafa: Fear is a natural reaction and if the individual buying a franchise does not have fear, it is not normal. I would caution anyone without fear to think twice about what they are doing and be sure they are fully informed and ready for owning all aspects of the business.

How does someone know when to start a business or buy a franchise?

Tafa: When an investor is ready to make a decision—be sensible, be cautious, fully vet the concept, and involve your spouse in the decision. You will want to make sure the demographics are in your favor and the work has intrinsic value. If you can check all the boxes you'll be ready to move forward.[18]

ARE YOU A MILITARY VETERAN?

Veterans bring a lot of transferable skills to a business, particularly to a franchised market, as they have learned how to follow systems and protocols.

I want to take a few paragraphs to address those of you who are veterans. Often, veterans have trouble transitioning to civilian life and can feel like they don't know how to fit in. In fact, veterans bring a lot to the table when it comes to running a business, and there are special resources available to help you, too.

Many veterans thrive as franchise business owners because many of the skills used in their service are the same skills needed to run a business. Both veterans and business owners need to have discipline, leadership skills, organizational skills, and must be willing to take responsibility for their actions. Also, their military experience prepares them to follow structured instructions. This experience relates well to supporting the methods and procedures set forth by the franchisor. Entrepreneurship allows veterans to leverage the skills obtained through their service in the military.

Veteran small business ownership helps drive our overall economy while providing our returning soldiers the opportunity to own a business. Cindy Bates states that according to the Small Business Administration (SBA), "Veterans are twice as likely to jump into entrepreneurship as civilians and about 20 percent of small business employees' work for veteran-owned businesses."[19]

There is an entrepreneurial program for veterans through the SBA called Boots to Business.[20] If you are a veteran, check out the resources and training available at the website at https://sbavets.force.com/s/ and the SBA Office of Veteran's Business Development at https://www.sba.gov/offices/headquarters/ovbd.

Another option for our veterans is the VetFran[21] initiative through the International Franchise Association (IFA), which encourages franchisors to offer discounts to veterans as a way to say "thanks" for their service and provide opportunities for business ownership. Several franchises offer franchise fee discounts and other incentives for veterans who invest in their concept.

Be sure to check with the SBA office for information on options for business loans specifically for veterans before making a commitment for financing. Remember, financing is a loan that must be paid back.

That is why you should list your veteran status as part of your profile and be thorough in identifying the skills you learned while serving. List also what you learned about your strengths and weaknesses. You may find you are better prepared to own a franchise than many of your peers who went the corporate route first.

Military veterans and athletes make great franchisees. They have demonstrable experience in following systems, finding motivation to do the work, and working hard—all critical factors to business success. Nonetheless, there are very successful business and franchise owners from all walks of life. If you do not fit into one of the above professions but are motivated and willing to learn, take heart—there almost certainly is a business or franchise for you.

ABILITY TO FOLLOW DIRECTIONS

One of the significant advantages of a franchise is the systems that are already in place. The methods provide a blueprint for your business. The policies and procedures have been tested and proven to work. The franchisor wants to find people who are ready and willing to follow the directions laid out by the franchise.

That's not to say they want a robot and there's no room for creativity or independent thinking, but whatever leeway you have is within the context of the franchise agreement and larger brand. We'll talk in a later chapter about how to factor this into your decision-making.

Willingness to Follow the Franchise System

One of the most common reasons for a franchisee's failure is that they did not follow the franchise system. It is widely-known that a true entrepreneur is probably not a good fit for a franchise because they will want to make changes to suit their personality or push their opinions about how to run the business. Franchises are set-up for franchisees to follow the methods and procedures that are developed through years of experience of the franchisor.

Brad Sugars, Founder, Chairman and President of ActionCOACH explains why it's important to follow the franchise system. He emphasizes you only need follow the system and methods already in place to see a healthy return on investment.

Unfortunately, if a franchisee makes changes because they think they are improving the brand, just the opposite is true. Making changes can hurt the brand and other franchisees. Sugars says, "it's important to remember that franchise systems are set up the way they are for a reason, and the reason is they work."[22]

As a franchisee, if you feel you need to make improvements to the business, you should ask for input from the franchisor and other franchisees. There is a good chance someone has been through the situation before and can assist with your ideas or offer another solution. Going back to the system for a solution is recommended before implementing any changes.

Americans are independent people when it comes to our ideas, insights, and experiences, and sometimes it looks more natural to follow a different path than the one laid out. However, if you're purchasing a franchise, you've already determined that this business has found a proven model for success. Why would you want to sabotage your own success by refusing to follow the model?

That said, it's important to research franchises that allow for some flexibility in local markets. Each area of the country varies greatly economically and demographically. Some franchises are more flexible than others. Be sure to ask about flexibility during your interviews with the company and current franchisees. What works well in one area of the country may not work well in yours.

Look for franchisors that communicate well and offer a product or service with profitable operations. How do you feel about your conversations with the franchisor? Do they have your best interests in mind? Do they care about their franchisees?

In 2008, Padgett Business Services celebrated their 40th year in business and more than 30 years in franchising. CEO Steven M. Rafsky explains that not much has changed in the decades-long core business offering. When looking at their history, they have determined that the most successful franchisees follow the entire system.[23]

It's essential for franchisees to buy into the entire system. Padgett's long-term success has proven that their well-defined system creates continuity throughout the company and supports everyone's success. They emphasize compliance with the system along with support and security to their franchisees. Through highlighting the benefits of continuity, franchisees benefit from a more predictable experience.

Rafsky points out the benefits of system-wide continuity. Who can step in if you become ill and cannot perform your operations? If you have system-wide procedures, it will be easier for someone from corporate or another franchisee to step in and help during a crisis. They need to follow the system that is laid out in the manual. Padgett did find that those who followed the entire system were the most profitable owners.

Paramount to running a successful franchise is following the franchise's systems. Commit to the policies, learn the steps and procedures, and follow them. When choosing a franchise, choose one that has well-written, easy to follow instructions and support. You are paying for the proven systems—utilize them every way you can. Those who do not follow the methods have no excuse for poor performance.

OPENNESS TO TRAINING

If you have many business experiences, you may think you do not need training. However, it is one of the most critical aspects of running your franchise business. Spend as much time as you can training, learning, and absorbing as much as possible. When you are in a classroom, it may seem tedious or overwhelming, however, when you are out in your territory, it will pay off in significant ways.

If you are so independent that you will want to go in and change the procedures or methods, a franchise is probably not for you. Some franchises are much stricter than others about their policies. A newer emerging brand will not be as stringent as a franchise that has been around a long time. Be sure to find out the type of franchise you will be working with and how much structure is required.

We have completed an overview of franchising and various forms of franchises and businesses and strategies to confront your fear of buying a business. In Step Four we will examine concrete steps to buying the right business.

I learned that courage was not the absence of fear, but the triumph over it. The brave man is not he who does not feel afraid, but he who conquers that fear.
—Nelson Mandela

STEP FOUR

YOUR BLUEPRINT FOR SELECTING A FRANCHISE

SELECT THE RIGHT BUSINESS

Now that you have a broad foundation in what a franchise is and you have practical strategies for pushing through your fear, it's time to figure out just how you select the right franchise business for you. Here in Step Four, I will share with you my six-stage process to help you make the right decision on franchise ownership. By taking time to evaluate your personal and business goals and exploring your options, you will go a long way to finding a business that is a good match for you. This process will help you find clarity in your search. If you are like others I have worked with, the "light bulb" will turn on and you will realize things about yourself you never considered before taking these steps.

When selecting a franchise business, you will need to confront your fears. You have to educate yourself, make a commitment to the process, and commit to making a decision.

As you take this journey of discovering which business is right for you, remind yourself of all the things we talked about in Step Two. Fear will rear its ugly head and try to derail you. Don't let it. Do your homework. Strategize a plan. Commit to pushing through your fears. Do not forget that everyone who starts a business deals with fear at some point. Be aware that fear and anxiety will happen and you can be prepared for it when it does, then move forward with your plans.

STAGE 1:
CREATE A PERSONAL PROFILE

No one can figure out your worth but you.
—Pearl Bailey

Similar to looking for a job. The first stage in finding the right business is to conduct a personal assessment. Spend time getting to know yourself, your business and lifestyle goals and ambitions. Better to spend a few hours creating a detailed profile than to spend your fortune on a business that does not suit you.

Similar to searching for a career or a job, assessing your skills and experiences are important. A résumé and or curriculum vitae (CV) will be helpful when putting together your list, as some topics will be the same or similar.

Education

Having a college degree is helpful, however, depending on your experiences and the type of business you are interested in, may not be necessary. List all your education, degrees, certifications, and courses of study, as these will help you identify interests and skills.

Occupation

List your occupations, your job titles, how long you held each position. Your overarching skills can bring a lot to the table. Always reflect upon how your experiences would help you run your business. You may think they do not relate; on the contrary, there are plenty of skills that transcend any particular industry and are transferable to other facets of life and business. For example: if your business would require you to train employees, you may not have experience training employees. However, experience teaching a class at church or to a community organization is a valuable experience that could transfer into training your employees.

Give thought to your various positions, even jobs you held while in college provide valuable experiences. Describe the jobs you have held and the skills you used, especially, skills that will help you run a business.

Create a list of the positives and negatives of jobs you have held.

Thinking about your likes and dislikes will help you avoid getting into a position you detest. Sometimes people think they should choose a business that is similar to their current job. However, if you do not like your current situation, what makes you think you will like owning a company doing the same work? Worry less about what's familiar and more about what gets you motivated.

Every job has positives and negatives. Is there something you honestly would never want to do again? Make sure the business you choose does not include this type of work or that you can afford to hire someone else to complete these unpleasant tasks.

List your strengths

Listing your strengths will help you define what you are good at doing. Look for businesses that play to your strengths. If you excel in a particular area, chances are you enjoy that type of work and it has some intrinsic value.

List your weaknesses

Even though your mom thinks you're perfect, the truth is you probably have some shortcomings, and when it comes to business, you want to be honest with yourself about them. Think about your weaknesses, those tasks where you struggle. If your business requires those tasks, will you be able to hire someone to do them for you? If not, you may want to reconsider your choice. If the industry consists of hiring employees, make sure to hire people who play to your strengths and fill in for your weaknesses.

List transferable skills for running a business

Take into account the skills that will transfer to running a business. Do you have computer skills, administrative skills, management skills? Are you skilled at finances, numbers, sales, or marketing? Are you organized? Everyone has talents, what are yours?

Write a list. Record everything you've ever done you were decent at doing, even if you would never put it on your resume—this list is for you, after all. You will be surprised if you dig deep into your experiences the number of skills you have developed throughout your education and career.

People skills

Every business requires working with customers and often employees. Outgoing people are often better at sales. I have talked to a lot of potential franchisees who say they are not good at sales and don't want to sell. If that is the case, you will probably need to hire someone to help you with sales or take a sales course. Some businesses involve consultative selling which may be a better fit. Reflect upon your comfort with sales and the type of sales you are willing to do when buying a business.

Customer service skills are a necessity. If you are afraid to talk with people, it will be challenging to run a successful business unless you pay someone else to do the talking for you. Paying a manager will take away from the bottom line, thus minimizing your profits.

How well do you get along with others? Do you enjoy working with different personalities? How about handling demanding customers or employees? Your success may depend upon your ability to deal with frustrating people and circumstances.

STAGE 2: DEFINE YOUR GOALS AND INTERESTS

After you have created your profile, it is time to mull over how your business fits in with your lifestyle and how it will meet your personal and professional goals. Whenever you are making life-changing decisions, you should write a thorough description of your goals and values. Conduct a self-reflection to identify your values and needs, in addition to performing an analysis of how your decisions will affect the people in your life. Who are the stakeholders in your life? Family, co-workers, friends. Ask yourself, do the franchise values coordinate with yours?

Keith TenBrook of Decision Making Solutions explains, "The underlying premise of effective decision making is that the decision maker knows their needs and desires. Risk becomes unbounded when this is *not* the case."[1]

Two types of goals

When you are writing your goals, make sure to use positive language. How we set goals can provide insight into our choices. According to Dr. Tsaousides[2], there are two types of goals: promotion and prevention. *Promotion goals* are positive: I want to get a raise. *Prevention goals* are the opposite: I don't want to lose my job. Table three provides guidance to help you align your goals.

People who use promotion goals are much more effective, while people who use prevention goals have more difficulty achieving their goals. Tsaousides goes on to say, "Fear of failure leads to the creation of prevention goals, which may blur our focus, undermine our efforts, and make planning difficult. Reframing prevention goals as promotion goals is one way to take the fear of failure out of the equation."[3]

As you set your goals, pay attention to how you word them. Prevention goals can make it harder to move forward and make it easier to give up. Avoid words like *don't, no, not, avoid, and never,* in favor of *earn, achieve, create, produce,* and other action words. Write down your goals and ambitions, and talk about them. The more you do this, the more likely it is you will reach them. Remember, people who use promotion (positive) goals are much more successful!

Table 3. Promotion vs. Prevention Goals
Road blocks to Achieving your Goals

Your vision POSITIVES: PROMOTION	Your fears NEGATIVES: PREVENTION
Motivation—why do I want to make this change?	Fear—what am I most afraid will happen?
List your POSITIVES of buying a franchise or business.	What is the likelihood that your fears will come true?
How can you prepare to buy the franchise or business where you will be successful?	What will you do if you don't take this step? Will you regret this decision?
Once you have made a decision, what steps will you take to fulfill your goals?	Once you have decided to move forward, what steps will you take to avoid your fears?

SMART Goal Setting

Everything we accomplish involves setting and achieving goals. We cannot do everything, so we need to prioritize how we use our time. Setting timelines for meeting goals is imperative to success. Using SMART goals, let's break down the process of accomplishing your business dream.

What is SMART goal setting? SMART is an acronym for: Specific, Measurable, Attainable, Relevant, and Timely. In what follows, I'll walk you through the process of setting SMART goals for your business.

SPECIFIC. Be specific about what you want to achieve. Write a description that details your business goals. Ask *who, what, when, where, why,* and *how* questions. You will also want to list possible alternatives to your goal.

An example of a specific goal is: I (who) want to own a cleaning business (what) in my community (where) that allows me time to spend with my family on weekends (why) and utilizes my management skills (what), by the end of this year (when). The reason I want to own my own business is that I want to have some control over the decisions made in my work (why). I will research franchise options (how) and decide by November this year (when).

An unspecified goal is: I want to own a franchise (or business).

MEASURABLE. You must be able to measure your progress and what it will be like when you reach your goals. Start with your end goal—what does it look like, what exactly is it.

You are faced with limitless choices. Defining where you want to end up will go a long way in narrowing your focus. Where do you want your business to take you? You are just getting started; however, it is helpful to take into account your ending objective. Is it your goal to run the business for a few years and sell it to retire? Perhaps you would like to build a business you can pass on to your children. Do you want to grow a large business and sell it in a few years and move on to something else? Is building the company to the point where you can be a semi-absentee or absentee owner your aspiration? Your end goal will determine the type of businesses you should examine.

Example: Say, my end goal is to build a business that I can sell in 10 years with enough money to retire. First, I will research business options and decide by November of this year. Second, I will open my business by January 1 of next year. Third, I will follow all of the systems laid out by the franchise or business and build the business. Fourth, I will work hard to grow the business following quarterly sales reports and increasing sales every quarter. Fifth, I will analyze my progress each month. Sixth, I will sell the company after ten years and have enough equity in the business to sell it with a profit of $500,000.

After you have described your end goal, break down the steps to get there. Measuring will help you define your goals and make it more apparent how you can reach them.

ATTAINABLE. Set goals that are attainable. Is it possible for you to reach this goal? If you do not have the finances, experience, or motivation to go through with the business, it is better, to be honest with yourself and choose a plan B.

Look at the opportunity cost of effort, time, your obligations, and other responsibilities to decide if it is attainable at this time. It may be better to wait a few years when you have the finances and time to devote full time to your business success.

Assuming you have the tools in your arsenal to move forward, set an attainable goal. It is probably not going to happen in the next week. However, if you allow a few months, it will surely be possible. Reach for the stars and remember you can adjust your goals as you go through the process. Planning carefully for your business will go a long way to helping you achieve your goals.

RELEVANT. Is this something you *want* to do? Is your goal relevant to you? Owning a business is a full-time job and requires juggling multiple tasks such as bookkeeping, social media, and advertising as well as customers, employees, inventories, and much more. Many people with businesses work 80–100-hour weeks. If buying a franchise, you can ask the current franchisees about their work hours to get an idea if they would suit your lifestyle. Do you have the personality for this type of business? Only you can decide, and this is where your assessment in stage one is beneficial. Ask yourself why you want to own your own business and what your objectives are for this business. Will running your own business achieve your goals?

You may be convinced that owning your own business will be fantastic, however, it would be best if you would talk with other owners to get an idea of the day-to-day, week-to-week, and year-to-year obligations. Find out the pros and cons of the businesses and use their feedback to help make a decision.

TIMELY. Setting deadlines triggers people to action. When students have a time frame for a paper due in school, they often put off working on it until the last minute—that deadline is what forces them to get it finished. Without a cutoff date, it will never get done.

It is the same with business and making other important decisions. Give yourself deadlines and make a significant effort to stick to them. That doesn't mean you can't adjust as you go and allow yourself some flexibility, but it will help put an endpoint to your thinking. Keep your timeline realistic so you can make sound decisions, not decisions made in haste.

When setting your goals, frame them positively, that is, in terms of what you will do. Focus on the positive and focus on your goals will significantly increase your chances of attaining them on time. Using SMART goals will give you clarity and improve your processes in business and life.

DEFINE YOUR INTERESTS

When you are not working, what do you like to do? In your spare time do you golf, ride horses, play video games, run, spend time with family, or watch TV? Are you interested in politics, entrepreneurship, the environment, or networking? What gets your heart pumping, your adrenaline going, and makes you happy? Are you obsessed with something you can't get out of your mind? Your interests are an essential part of you, and they can lead you to good career and business choices.

Create a list of your interests and examine how they might be related to a business. If you like dogs, there are many businesses that relate to dogs and animals. You may want to think about a grooming, kenneling, training, or supplies business. If you enjoy small business, there are coaching options that help entrepreneurs grow their businesses. If you enjoy being around children, there are multiple options for tutoring, childcare, and STEM lessons. Are you an avid runner or exercise enthusiast, perhaps opening a gym or personal training business would be a great option? The possibilities are varied, unique, and number in the thousands. Defining your interests will help you find a business that suits your style.

Hobbies as a business

While it is great to work in a business you have a passion for; I would like to give a heads-up to beware of a business that is centered on your favorite pastime.

I have a friend (let's call her Susie), who loved to golf. It offered her socialization, challenge, and exercise. Susie loved golfing so much she thought she wanted to own a business where golfing was an integral part of the company. She started working at a golf course teaching lessons and helping customers.

I saw her a couple of years later and asked her how her golfing was going. She said, "I do not play golf anymore; golfing is not fun for me. I am here all the time, and I am tired of it."

It happens more than you might think. Someone wants to combine business with their favorite leisure pursuit, however, after working at it 40–80 hours a week, they do not have time for their hobby, or they lose interest. It becomes a job rather than a recreation. Be sure to consider this possibility before choosing a business that might spoil your hobby. You might want to find something where you can be successful and allows you time to enjoy your favorite hobby in your spare time.

FALLING IN LOVE WITH THE FIRST FRANCHISE

Terry saw a franchise that she felt was perfect for her. She imagined completing the day-to-day tasks and managing her employees, and it felt right. Fortunately, she went through the 6-step process I outlined in this book, which led her to change her mind. After comparing this particular franchise with another one, Terry realized the second one was a much better fit because it played better to her skillset and had excellent franchisor support. Terry is happy with her decision and is very glad she did not go with her first choice. Getting to know herself and learning about her selected franchises saved her from living a life of misery.

Most people do not go with their first choice of business; once they start looking wholeheartedly at options, they often find another alternative is a better fit. Often individuals come to me with a franchise in mind. However, after learning about their options, the majority of the time they choose something different. Don't be surprised if this happens to you.

KEY FEATURES

Are there essential elements and components you feel you have to have in your business? If you are looking for a job, you will want to create a list of the benefits and features of the position. When buying a home, everyone has features they want in the home, for example, location, size, affordability, bathrooms, new or used. Just as you would when buying a home, make a list of the elements that are very important for your business.

Be mindful of the following characteristics of any business and be aware of how they impact your decisions.

Economic. There must be an economic activity that benefits customers by satisfying a want or need. What about employees? Do you want to build a team, or would you prefer to work alone? Building a business where you hire employees is beneficial to the economy and helps other people while working solo can be very rewarding and less stressful than hiring employees.

Product or service. What product or service will you sell? Are there products or services that you are very interested in providing? Explore those that interest you the most. There must be a market demand—or in the case of a new business, there should be a problem that lacks a current solution. Think about the challenges of supplying this product or service. It helps if you are passionate or are interested in the product or services you will provide.

Profit motive. A business must have a way to bring in more income than it pays out in expenses. Understand how you will make a profit and how long it will take to show a return on investment. Profit is required for a business to grow and expand. Without income, the company dies. Studying the FDD, talking to the franchisor and franchisees and an accountant will help you determine the potential profit of the business.

Risk. What is your level of risk tolerance? Categorize it as high-, medium-, or low-level. Take your level of risk tolerance into consideration when purchasing a franchise. Newer, emerging franchises have a higher chance of risk because of the lack of historical data. However, developing brands can provide the opportunity to get in on the ground floor of a growing trend. Franchises that have a long history and franchises that offer lower risk usually command a higher cost. Investigate how resilient this business would be in a recession. The product or service will provide key factors into the recession-resistance.

Financial. One of the most important factors in choosing a business is finding one that you can afford.

Franchise start-up outlay ranges from $10,000–$3,000,000. The average franchise investment is $100,000–$150,000. You will pay the franchise an upfront franchise fee and typically royalties each week or month. Other than that, the cost of doing business is about the same as starting a business from scratch.

Minimum financial requirements. It's essential that the franchisee meet the minimum requirements for financing. Most franchisors require a minimum net worth. The reason for a net worth requirement is that lack of capital is the number one reason small businesses fail. The franchisor wants you to be successful and adequately prepared for the first few months. So should you!

The minimum requirements are the result of the franchises past practices. The investment information is valuable to you as a franchisee since it helps you know what to expect. Many people make the mistake of reading the franchise fee without realizing there are many more expenses in the initial investment (see FDD, Item 7). Financial surprises are not fun when starting a business. Study the industry, your local market, and talk with other franchisees for further input.

Financing options. There are many options for financing your business, and sometimes even the franchisor has financing available. Due to the positive track record of franchises, the Small Business Administration works with banks to offer a loan guarantee program for certain franchises that have a good past performance with franchisees. There are several financial professionals that specialize in franchise loans, who can help you calculate reasonable minimum financial preparedness. You will also need a business plan if you are asking for a loan to fund your business. The Small Business Administration provides information on writing a business plan at https://www.sba.gov/tools/business-plan/1 on their website. You can get help with writing your business plan, make sure you know what is in it so that you can follow through.

In addition, alternative means for financing exist, including 401K and IRA rollovers. When set up correctly, utilizing your retirement funds for a business does not incur tax penalties. Talk to your franchise consultant or the franchisor for recommendations.

Undercapitalization. One of the most common reasons businesses fail is due to undercapitalization. You may think you have enough capital to make it through to positive cash flow. However, it often takes longer than anticipated to get started and begin seeing a return on investment. Plan for several months of start-up before bringing home a salary. Having extra cash available as a cushion will see you through rough patches. If it turns out you do not need it that is even better. If a spouse continues working while you work on your business, their income will help alleviate worries about paying the bills. Read the investment section of the FDD (Items 5, 6, 7) carefully as it lists items and costs needed for start-up. A good financial plan is the best way to avoid undercapitalization.

Creativity. How much does use of creativity factor into your ideal business? Some businesses thrive on creativity and innovation; others would prefer you follow the system accurately and do not waver. When buying a franchise, try to gauge the amount of creativity the franchisor permits—and whether it is tolerated or actually encouraged.

Franchisors realize that location demographics differ and generally make room for you to add your own local flavor. Yes, you need to follow the franchise's systems. However, there are other aspects in which you will be free to make decisions such as who to hire and fire and how you handle local marketing. You may also have input into any changes that corporate wants to make. Again, the franchisor wants you to be successful, which means you have to be successful in your locale.

Customers. What type of customers do you prefer? Would you prefer to work with consumers or businesses? If you enjoy children or senior citizens, you may want to think about one of the many options in these fields. If your desire is to serve businesses, plenty of options exist. There are pros and cons to each, accordingly, and it often comes down to personal preferences. However, your product or services need to focus on customer satisfaction and quality, so it helps if you actually like your customers.

Environmental or social consciousness. Businesses now are expected to be ecologically and socially conscious. How will your business fit into this scenario? Many franchises are taking the environment into account with the use of environmentally safe products. Others are making strides towards socially conscious donations. If these factors are important to you, look for a business that will satisfy this goal.

Type of business. There are many types of companies. Do you prefer a retail establishment? Would going to people's homes and providing a valuable service interest you? Do you want to service or sell products to other businesses? Businesses are frequently put into categories depending upon the hours required, the customers served, and the requirements for space. A retail store is an expensive investment due to the costs of lease space and inventory expenses. On the other hand, a home-based service business enjoys less costly overhead. Perhaps you would enjoy a business where you drive a service van from place to place.

These attributes are important factors in choosing a business or franchise. Take some time to answer these questions and reflect on their impact on your goals. Table four will help you rate the franchises as you are narrowing your search. This table will assist in making a knowledgeable decision by ranking the attributes. Add your own essential features to this list and rank those as well.

Table 4. Franchise Rating Worksheet
Rate franchises 1–5 for each item with 5 being the highest.

PRODUCT/SERVICE CONSIDERATIONS	Rating 1-5	MANAGEMENT TEAM QUESTIONS	Rating 1-5	TYPE OF BUSINESS	Rating 1-5	MARKETING AND FRANCHISOR SUPPORT	Rating 1-5
Equipment costs (low-high)		Company backing (good-excellent)		B2B (Prefer working with businesses?)		Is there grand opening support? How much?	
Footprint required (lease)		Experience with this product or service?		Consumers (Prefer working with consumers?)		Ongoing support? How much?	
Is the Product Trendy? New?		Franchising experience?		Economic viability and Rate of Growth		What percent of sales are franchisees expected to spend on advertising?	
Investment all-in (low-high)		Units (is the franchise growing or losing units?)		Kind of clients (middle-class, professionals, upper-middle class?)		Type of marketing provided	
Operation (simple-challenging)		How much training is provided?		Revenues recurring?		Social media support	
Product/ Service cost (low-high)		Profitability of the business model?		Location type (home based, industrial, retail)		Advertising (National funds or Local?)	
Intrinsic value to you as owner— to your customers		Area developers or representatives available?		Employees? (Skilled, unskilled) How many?		Advertising Costs/Types	
Proven concept (years in business)		Territory Size		Ownership? (absentee, semi-absentee, manager/ owner run)			
Totals							

Are You a Pioneer?

According to the Free Dictionary, the definition of a pioneer is "1) One who ventures into an unknown or unclaimed territory to settle or 2) One who opens up new areas of thought, research or development."[4] A franchise pioneer introduces a new concept—either a new business that can be franchised or a way to franchise a business that was previously independent.

From time to time a new a product or service becomes available that pioneers an industry. For those that are enterprising and adventurous, the opportunity to enter a pioneering market can be the chance of a lifetime. An emerging market offers exciting new challenges, the adventure of trying something new, and the promise of great success.

Each year I discover a few franchise concepts that are pioneers in their industries and stand out from the crowd. Are you interested in emerging brands? Perhaps you are looking for the challenge of growing a pioneering business? One of the best places to find out about these new franchises is to check with a franchise consultant since they are the first to find out about new franchise options.

STAGE 3:
NARROW YOUR OPTIONS

If you are working with a franchise consultant, narrowing your options will be much easier than working alone. The consultant will use your personal profile to choose two or three options that are a good fit using the information from conversations and your profile.

If you are researching on your own, your search will require many hours. If you enjoy having salespeople call you at all hours, searching on the World Wide Web to find a franchise will be quite fun. Since everyone I know dislikes having their time disrupted by pushy salespeople, you should seriously consider working with a franchise consultant. Again, there is typically no fee for their services since they are retained by the franchise companies to find qualified candidates.

The personal summary you created can help you identify the characteristics you want in your business, and from there you can narrow down your search to the kinds of franchises that satisfy your requirements. Don't worry yet about whether your requirements are "too strict"; there are a bewildering amount of different franchise models out there, so trust the process.

To narrow your options, consider the factors discussed in Stages 1 and 2. List what you must have in your business and answer the following questions about your preferred lifestyle.

How active do you plan to be in your business?

Are you planning to keep your job and run the business part-time? Franchisors typically prefer that the franchisee act as the face of the business and is on-site running the day-to-day operations. However, some franchises allow absentee or semi-absentee ownership. A semi-absentee or absentee business will permit you to work your current job until you can transition into the company full time. Many people keep their franchise as a side business and do both. Be sure to investigate your options. If you are looking for passive or semi-passive income, choose a franchise that is specifically set up to meet your goals.

If you prefer a semi-absentee or absentee business, the options will be more limited. You may need to hire someone else to manage the business on a day-to-day basis, which means additional staffing costs. Also, remember a manager will not have the same investment in building the company as you the owner will.

Are you a loner or team builder?

Do you want to work solo or do you desire employees? Many franchises are home-based, single operation, and you may be the kind of person who would enjoy working alone. However, there are plenty of larger companies if you want to hire employees and manage a more extensive operation.

What type of employees do you want to work within your business? Would you prefer highly skilled employees, or would you be fine working with less-skilled or unskilled lower-cost employees?

Do you prefer fixed or flexible working hours?

What kind of hours would you prefer to work? Is your preference Monday through Friday, 8 a.m. to 5 p.m.? Perhaps retail hours, seven days a week early morning through late at night are okay with you? These questions will dictate the type of business that will help you achieve your ideal lifestyle goals.

As you can see, there are many factors to think about when choosing a business or franchise. Take the time to go through the list in Table 4 and think about what you really want in a business.

Once you have decided what you truly want in a franchise, you can start searching for franchises that fit your criteria. A franchise that fits your specifications is like finding a needle in a haystack. The majority of options will not fit the bill, so you will need to either call every franchise you think you are interested in or search the Internet for their requirements.

In the previous stages, you reflected on who you are and how your ideal business would look. You spent hours and hours combing through franchise options, talking with your franchise consultant, attorney and accountant, and learning about franchises. Now you have made it so far as to narrow your choice to one or two options and the real decision making begins.

STAGE 4:
EXPLORE YOUR OPTIONS

Now that you've got a good sense of who you are and what your ideal business might look like, it's time to get out there and see what some actual franchise operations look like.

If you are working with a franchise consultant, they will provide you with information on two or three franchises that are a good fit based on your profile. This franchise information is an advantage to your search because the consultant is familiar with the options that are available. They will limit your options based on your financial capabilities, territory availability, and your personal and professional objectives.

The resources that are available for a franchise consultant are not readily open to the public, so they can help you avoid franchises that may be having internal or other issues. Besides, if a particular territory is not available, there is no point in wasting your time looking at an option that is not available where you want to locate. Your franchise consultant will complete a territory check before presenting you with options, thus avoiding that scenario.

Each franchise has its own process for screening candidates. Follow the steps in their process to get the most out of it and increase your chances of being awarded a franchise.

Questions for the franchisor

Create a spreadsheet in your program of choice. Along the side, list questions to ask and items to find out about each franchise (see Table 4). Then list each new franchise you investigate along the top and fill out the corresponding questions. You will want to ask the franchise developer several questions about their franchise, the management team, and their support of franchisees, and it will be important to keep them all straight, even if it's only a handful.

Stay open to possibilities

Take time with each option, and keep an open mind. Many franchise candidates I see are not as enthusiastic about my recommended possibilities for them as I am. However, once they take the time to learn about the franchise, their eyes are opened. Spend your time looking at it from the view of an owner rather than that of an employee. Tell yourself you are getting an education and you will always learn a great deal if you keep your ears and eyes open to the opportunities.

According to Terry Powell who wrote in *Entrepreneur.com*, "If you only look at businesses in an area where you are familiar or are good at, you place yourself at a major disadvantage by ignoring a huge number of possibilities that are outside your realm of past business experience."[5]

Franchise Interviews

An essential step in your search is when you talk with the franchisor. It is important to be aware of the significance of your interviews with the various people for whom you will come into contact. You will probably want to talk with the franchisor as soon as you narrow your options. There will be numerous calls with the franchisor and their various departments, with each call taking you further into the process.

Sometimes people considering a franchise assume that every franchisor will want them to own one of their franchises as long as they have the financial means. However, if you consider the franchisor's perspective, this is not the case. Think of it this way: would you want just anyone to be your child's nanny just because they came cheap? No, you would want someone with specific qualifications, a certain temperament, and with whom you could see yourself working. While capital is essential when buying a business, you must remember it is not all about money. Franchisors want franchisees that are going to be successful—their success is your success and vice versa. There may be a few franchises that will take "anyone," but I would advise you to stay away from this type of franchise. If a franchise does not thoroughly screen their applicants, there may be something wrong with their business model and you will want to complete a thorough investigation.

Tips for the initial call

A critical element of your investigation is the franchise interview. The first call is typically a get-to-know-you call with the franchise developer. If you are both comfortable after the first call, you may be asked to fill out an application.

As the franchisee, you want this company to want you as much as you want them. It is a mutual process. They do not take everyone. Franchises may receive hundreds (or even thousands) of inquiries for any given franchise. For example, *Chick-fil-a* receives more than 20,000 applicants per year. Below are some tips to keep in mind when talking with the franchisors.

Prepare for the franchise interview

Prepare for each encounter with the franchisor the same as you would prepare for a job interview. This interview is a mutual process—you are trying to see if you want to work with this franchise, just as you want to ensure you wanted to work for a prospective employer. The employer or franchisor wants to know if you are a good fit for their system, for their workplace.

Look for mutual benefits

Learn as much as you can about the company (employer or franchise). Explore their website, find some articles about them. Look for shared interests and ways that you may be able to contribute to the success of the company. They have a franchise business that you want to own. Show them the skills you have to offer as their franchisee.

Put your best foot forward

When going for an interview, you need to put your best foot forward. Be prepared, be ready and on time, and have well thought out questions ready at hand. If you had an interview scheduled and didn't show up or kept changing the time for the meeting, you would not seem very interested in the job—it is the same with a franchise interview. Not taking scheduled calls is a red flag for the franchise.

Show enthusiasm

Show enthusiasm! This business opportunity will change your life; if you are not excited about the concept or the company, how can you hope to do well owning it? Franchisors and employers alike look for drive and enthusiasm; they want people who want to be there and do what it takes to make the company successful.

One franchisor told me about a prospective franchisee (I'll call him Joe) who went through all of the steps to buy the franchise business and seemed like a good fit. Joe had the money to invest in the industry, and he met their qualifications. However, when Joe attended Discovery Day (a day to visit the franchise headquarters and meet the team), he seemed disinterested; he did not ask any questions and did not seem to care. Consequently, Joe was not offered a franchise. The development team did not feel that Joe was motivated enough to do well with their franchise.

If you are going to run a business, you should be excited and motivated to do well. You will need to be enthused and inspired to follow through and carry out the operations of the business.

By the same token, Marcus Lemonis suggests that prospective franchisees (i.e., *you*) should look for passion in the franchisor as well. You may be working together for a decade or more, so you'll want to work with a passionate team.

FOLLOW THE STEPS

I've mentioned this one before, but I'll say it again because it's so important. As a franchisee, you'll be expected to follow systems and protocols for running your business, so demonstrate your capacity for that by following the steps in the franchise application process carefully. Employers and franchisors alike have many steps a person must go through to determine their fit for a company.

Often there is an initial phone call, then two or three separate interviews. There may be a webinar about the company and other informational sessions. These are all necessary steps that help determine if a potential franchisee is the best choice. Each franchisor has a predetermined number of steps in the process. Before moving to the next level, each step must be completed to the franchisor's satisfaction. If you seem in a hurry and try to skip a step or two, the franchise may decide you cannot follow their procedures and are not a good fit.

As you move through each step, think of it as a milestone, and by the time you reach a final decision, you should know the company and its culture very well. Again, this is a life-changing decision—don't rush into it. You want this company to want you as much as you want them. By preparing for the franchise interview, putting your best foot forward, learning as much as you can, showing enthusiasm and following the steps you will have done all you can to position yourself for success with that franchise. In turn, you will have given the franchisor the best opportunities to be candid and open with you, and thus you will learn more and be more confident in your final choice.

Remember, not everyone is suited for every job or every franchise. It's better to learn that your favorite choice is a bad fit during this step than after rushing into buying the business and being miserable a year in. Take your time here and don't hesitate to ask all the questions you have until you get all the answers you need. If at any time you get nervous and need help, your professional consultant will help you walk through the process and answer questions.

STAGE 5:
CONDUCT A THOROUGH REVIEW

Fortune favors the prepared mind.

—Louis Pasteur

With thousands of franchises in the United States, choosing a franchise is no small task. It can feel like finding a needle in a haystack. Careful preparation will pay off in big ways in the future of your business. Once you have chosen one or two franchises, you will want to do a thorough review of the franchise before making your final choice.

Due Diligence

An essential step in your search for the right business or franchise is conducting *due diligence*. According to Wikipedia, "*Due diligence* is an investigation of a business or person prior to signing a contract, or an act with a certain standard of care."[6] When you are buying a franchise, there are many factors to take into account.

Conducting due diligence through quality information gathering and thorough investigation will go a long way to reflective decision making, minimizing risk and promoting positive outcomes. You will also want to talk with a franchise attorney, and an accountant as part of your analysis. When purchasing a franchise, be sure to look carefully at the agreement and obtain legal and financial advice before committing.

Missed Opportunities

It is possible to *due diligence* yourself out of anything, that is, to be so particular and risk-averse that you exclude every actual, real-life business *before* you've begun exploring. I have worked with people who have done precisely that. They won't even give consideration to some options because of something someone said, did, or mentioned about the opportunity. These are missed opportunities. Don't overanalyze your choices or you will never realize your dreams. Overanalyzing can turn into *analysis paralysis*, and you will never make a decision.

If you want to own a business, look for one that you can agree with 80–90%. It is very rare for someone to be 100% sold on a franchise or business option, however, if you feel 80–90% agreeable, then odds are in your favor. Acknowledge what you will be comfortable with, buy a business you'll be proud of, and forget about being perfect.

Due Diligence and Review

Following are six essential items to include on your review of the franchise. Be sure to ask questions about these factors.

Longevity. How many years has the franchise been in business? Many times a company will exist for several years before becoming a franchise. The longer the company has been franchising, the more information you will be able to glean from their experience. As a franchise matures, their systems and processes evolve as well. Therefore, the longer a franchise has been in business, the higher likelihood of franchisee satisfaction and success. If you have a low-risk tolerance, you may want to look at franchises that have been around several years.

The number of units/locations. How many franchises are there? How many sites are open? More units means more brand recognition, more marketing expenditures, and more franchisees. There are exceptions to this since emerging brands with few locations offer separate challenges and advantages.

Systems, procedures, and operations. Are the systems, processes, and operations well-written and easy to follow and implement? Are the expectations set forth by the franchisor reasonable and attainable? How do current franchisees feel about the methods already in place?

Support from the franchisor. Find out about assistance with marketing and advertising, training, and continuing education. Exactly what type of support and how much training will be provided?

The culture of the organization. Are you comfortable with the culture and core values of the organization? Can you work with this group of people for the length of the contract, anywhere from 5–20 years? How are the other franchisees doing? What is the relationship with franchisees?

Take the matter of core values seriously. Do the core values of the franchise correlate with your own? If not, you should probably walk away. You want to be allied with a company that treats people well, values their customers, and has the best interests of the franchisee in mind. If you're getting a bad vibe, better not to get financially entangled with that company.

Validation from franchisees. Talking with existing franchisees is one of the most beneficial aspects of buying a franchise. You will want to speak with several franchisees. As a courtesy be sure to ask the franchisor which franchisees you can call. This is not the time to be shy—we're talking about your future.

Create a list of questions to ask before calling the franchisee. Be sure to ask what their typical day is like to get an idea of what you will be doing day to day. Spend time talking with current and former franchise owners to get their take on the franchise. Find out what they like and what they do not like about the business. Try not to spend too much of any one franchisee's time. Remember, they are busy running a business!

Beware of the bad apple. The cliché goes, "One bad apple spoils the bunch." Sometimes, a franchisee may be the bad apple through no fault of the franchisor. Maybe they don't get along, or perhaps the franchisee failed for some reason other than something the franchisor did. Do not give up just because you heard one or two negative comments. It seems the ones who have complaints talk the loudest, while the satisfied franchisees are too busy building their business to complain. If you hear one tale of woe, you might have a bad apple situation. That's why you should talk to several franchisees. If many of them are unhappy, there may be a concern that you need to check out further.

Realize that every day in business is not wonderful, and when you are talking to franchisees, they may be having a bad day. They may be in a hurry or just do not want to bother talking about their business. Keep this in mind as they are taking time out of their day to speak with you.

I have had potential franchisees discontinue their search merely because they heard one or two negative comments and assumed the entire franchise is terrible. What a shame, to miss out on an excellent opportunity without getting both sides of the story. It makes me think of reading a negative review on *Yelp*! about a restaurant or business. I have to remind myself that one negative review should not keep me from doing business with them. I might miss out on a great experience.

Talk with all levels of performers

The franchisor will want to show off his or her best-performing franchisees, and you should definitely ask them what they are doing to perform so well. Use this information to become high-performing yourself. In addition, seek out low-performing franchisees and see if you can find out why they are low-performing. More than likely, it is not about the franchise but lack of management skills, poor location, or other factors. You can ask the franchisor to give you a list of franchisees with various performance from low to high and somewhere in the mid-range. This way you can be sure you are talking to franchisees that are not just the higher-level performers.

Franchisee satisfaction

Interview current franchisees and ask about their satisfaction with the franchisor. If the franchisees are happy and would do it again, the franchise is probably a good bet. Happy franchisees make more money and value their business. This validation is essential and will give a good insight into the culture of the franchise and the success of franchisees. Do not skip this step!

EXAMINING THE FDD

The FDD, or Franchise Disclosure Document, is a disclosure document that provides information about a franchise for the prospective franchisee, which is required by the Federal Trade Commission. The FDD is required to be delivered to you at least two weeks before you sign the franchise agreement. The FDD is a very long document, some of them are up to 300 pages long.

An FDD contains background information about the company and lists 23 items that cover just about everything you need to know about the franchise. You will want to check out the FDD soon after your initial call as it is an important document for franchisees and franchisors. You can locate the full text of the requirements in an FDD from https://ftc.gov.

Below is a brief summary of items on the FDD:

Item 1 – Franchisor. Gives a brief overview of the company; tells you how long the franchisor has been in business, provides the names of the franchisor, their predecessors, and their affiliates. It also states the aim of the franchisor's business and their experience.

Item 2 – Business Experience of Executives. Identifies the executives of the franchise system and describes their experience.

Item 3 – Litigation History. States if there is any relevant criminal or civil litigation regarding the company or its management. This item will tell you whether the franchisor or any of its executives have been held liable for—or settled civil actions involving—the franchise relationship.

Item 4 – Bankruptcy. Discloses whether the franchisor or its predecessor, affiliates or any of its executives have been involved in a recent bankruptcy. If the franchisor or its predecessor or affiliate has declared bankruptcy, carefully review the franchisor's financial statements in Item 21 of the FDD to see if the franchisor is financially capable of delivering the support services it promises. Consider having an accountant review the required financial statements too.

Item 5 – Initial Franchise Fee. Describes the amount the franchisee must pay to acquire the franchise as well as any deposits or franchise fees that may be non-refundable and how the franchisor settled on this amount.

Item 6 – Other Fees. Includes fees other than the initial franchise fee, including royalties, training fees, advertising contributions, licenses, salaries, and transfer and renewal fees. There may be additional fees that are not required to be disclosed such as the cost of products. You will want to ask about any undisclosed costs that are involved.

Item 7 – The Initial Investment. Contains a table with the estimated initial investment the franchisee must make to set up the business (including initial franchise fee, real estate, equipment and supplies, signs, advertising, and working capital), as well as when and how to make these payments. Keep in mind; these are estimates, and additional working capital may be needed. You'll need to investigate other initial and ongoing costs that aren't described in Items 5-7, such as the cost of accounting and legal help.

Item 8 – Restrictions on Sources of Products and Services. Describes restrictions on suppliers, products, equipment, or services related to the franchise. They may want you to only buy products from them or specific vendors. This specificity is what keeps consistency in products and equipment throughout the organization.

Item 9 – Franchisee's Obligations. This is a list of the franchisee's contractual obligations which refers to other sections of the agreement and the FDD. Read carefully as this item details what protocols you as a franchisee are required to follow.

Item 10 – Financing. States whether or not the franchisor offers to finance you. If so, the terms are included here. Some franchises offer to finance and work with third parties to assist their franchisees in obtaining financing.

Item 11 – Franchisor's Assistance, Advertising, Computer Systems, and Training. Includes wide-ranging information about the franchise system's advertising programs and the initial and ongoing training they will provide.

Item 12 – Territory. States if the franchisee is granted exclusive rights to territory and whether the franchisor can set up another unit within it.

Item 13 – Trademarks. Sets out the franchisor's trademarks, service marks, and trade names used.

Item 14 – Patents, Copyrights, and Proprietary Information. Contains information on which of these the franchisee may use and how.

Item 15 – Obligation to participate in the Operation of the Franchised Business. States whether the franchisee must be a hands-on owner or if you may be an absentee owner.

Item 16 – Restrictions on What the Franchisee May Sell. States the products or services the franchisee may sell.

Item 17 – Renewal, Termination, Transfers, and Dispute Resolution. Consists of a table that sets the terms of the agreement including the length of the term, renewals, termination reasons, transfer rights, and other items. Item 17 also explains what your obligations would be to the franchisor after termination.

Item 18 – Public Figures. Lists the names of any public figures that may be involved in the venture and the details of the celebrity's agreement.

Item 19 – Financial Performance Representations. Statement that contains what other franchises have earned also called an Earnings Claim. Nancy Lanard describes a franchise earnings claim as "any information provided to a prospective franchisee that allows that individual to predict the earnings or revenue that he/she can generate from the franchise business."[7] It is important to note that the franchisor is not required to provide an Earnings Claim. The salesperson, consultant, broker, or franchisor is only authorized to state numbers disclosed in the FDD.

Item 20 – Outlets and Franchisee Information. Provides information about other franchisees, company-owned outlets, the estimated number of franchises to be sold in the next year, and additional information. The charts show growth and owner turnover in the franchisor's system.

Item 21 – Financial Statements. Provides audited financial statements of the franchisor for the past three years.

Item 22 – Agreements. Includes the franchise agreement and any other contracts. The agreement contains additional information about the franchise and what you are agreeing to. You will want to read the agreement carefully, so you understand how it will affect your business.

Item 23 – Confirmation. Contains a receipt that you must sign, which states that the franchisor provided you with the FDD.[8] The franchisor will ask you to sign the confirmation as soon as you receive the FDD. By signing the confirmation, you are only saying that you received it. Since you are to have the agreement for two weeks before signing to buy the franchise, the franchisor needs confirmation of when you received the FDD.

The FDD is a legal document!

Thinking of skimming the FDD? Think again. The Franchise Disclosure Document (FDD) is a crucial component of your legal and financial relationship with the franchisor. Do not assume you know what is written there. Have a qualified franchise attorney go over the details of the legal document with you, so you understand the implications of what it contains.

You should go through the FDD and agreement carefully and make a note of questions you may have. If you are not clear on all items, check with the franchisor for clarification. Going over the FDD may feel like a chore; however, the FDD is a document provided to protect you and the franchisor from misunderstandings and disagreements in the future.

Obtaining the financial advice of an accountant is also recommended before making a commitment. Get to know the franchise well before signing the agreement.

Buying a franchise is a life-changing decision, be sure to conduct an extensive legal and financial investigation of your choice. Knowledge and education are powerful tools when opening a business or buying a franchise.

STAGE 6:
MAKE YOUR DECISION

It always seems impossible until it is done.
—Nelson Mandela

The hardest part of all is making the final decision. However, it's also the most exciting aspect because it's the moment when all your work pays off. You have created your profile, analyzed your options, conducted due diligence on your top two or three, and now it is time to make a decision.

By this time, your head is swimming with information, thoughts, and ideas. Try not to get overwhelmed with cognitive overload. You are probably very excited about your options and the one you will choose. You should have a pretty good idea which franchise is the right one for you. What do you do when indecision is blocking you from realizing your dreams? Step back and analyze your concerns and fears. Take action by following the strategies outlined in this book. No one can make this decision except you!

If you are still struggling to make a choice, keep reading. The next section provides you with tools and processes that you can use to complete this or any decision step.

If you don't go after what you want, you'll never have it. If you don't ask, the answer is always no. If you don't step forward, you're always in the same place.

—Nora Roberts

STEP FIVE

YOUR DIY DECISION-MAKING TOOLBOX

In previous sections of this book, I covered the history and basic facts about franchising, ways to work through the fear of opening a business, the steps to finding a suitable franchise or business, and some pitfalls of business ownership. In this section, I want to provide you with several tools and tips that you can use along your journey to make a knowledgeable decision. Feeling confident in your decision goes a long way to set yourself up for success.

MAKING A KNOWLEDGEABLE DECISION

Four steps to achievement: Plan purposefully. Prepare prayerfully. Proceed positively. Pursue persistently.
—William A. Ward

Using decision-making tools, intuition, and guidance, your business journey will be less stressful.

Another source of research, Decision Innovation. com provides individuals, consumers, and businesses with information and services on making informed decisions. Their extensive website contains articles, activities, graphs, and tips on decision making. The article "Making Effective Decisions in High Uncertainty," written by Keith TenBrook, explains that there is always uncertainty in decision making and discusses ways to change your decision making when you are uncertain about the outcomes:

The recurring theme for uncertain times is gaining knowledge. Knowledge provides the basis for security and familiarity. Decisions provide the framework for acquiring the knowledge that will reduce uncertainty and enable change.[1]

THE "NEARLY FLAWLESS" DIAMOND

Are you shopping for the perfect business? Unfortunately, just like the perfect diamond, the perfect business does not exist. You can spend countless hours in your search trying to discover a flawless franchise, and you will never find it.

When couples are shopping for the perfect diamond, their options vary according to the shape, color, clarity, cost, and size. The key is to search for the one that makes them happy, the one that is right for them. Those looking for a franchise would do well to think of their potential franchise as a "nearly flawless" diamond. Look, it's still a *diamond*!

While there are no perfect spouses or partners, there are no perfect businesses. I've worked with potential franchisees who always find something wrong, no matter how minute it may be. If they see one thing they don't agree with, they stop investigating altogether. How many couples would be married if they had decided to wait until they met the "perfect" person before taking their vows? Would there be franchisors with hundreds or thousands of franchisees if they waited for the "perfect" franchisee? I think not.

DETERMINE YOUR DECISION-MAKING STYLE

Your life changes the moment you make a new, congruent, and committed decision.
—Tony Robbins

It's hard to admit, but I, too, have difficulty making decisions. From choosing where to eat, what to eat, what car to buy, and what to do next, it can be problematic. Indecision is very frustrating to me (and my spouse). However, unless I have exhausted all options on the menu and researched the calorie count, I just can't bring myself to commit. When buying a car, I need to drive several, ask a hundred questions, peruse the consumer reviews, and find the best price and color before making a decision. I have been known to drive a car salesman batty, and once a realtor quit taking my calls because I couldn't decide on a house! There are times that I choose not to make a decision at all, rather than make the wrong choice. More often than not, when some time has gone by, I regret my procrastination because I lost out on something that was important to me.

Knowing this about myself, however, means I can plan ahead when I need to make a crucial decision. I can give myself time to do the research, ask my questions, and spend some quality time mulling it over *before* any deadlines.

How do *you* make important decisions in your life? When you have a choice to make, what steps do you take? Do you become paralyzed and end up not deciding at all? Most people ask someone else for their opinion on a topic. Who is your go-to person for decisions? Your spouse, a sibling, a parent, a co-worker, a professional? Is your go-to person supportive and positive? Think through your process.

Summarizing a study by Dan LaVallo and Oliver Sibony in the *McKinsey Quarterly*, the *Harvard Business Review* explained that there are five main decision-making styles among business leaders: Visionary, Guardian, Motivator, Flexible, and Catalyst.[2] I have determined that I am a Guardian, meaning I am conservative about risk and change and have a "strong preference for making decisions after exhaustive deliberation." That is, decision-making can literally exhaust me. For people who are Visionary or Catalyst in orientation, however, decision-making is energizing.

Understanding how you make decisions can help you define your strengths and weaknesses. By determining strengths and weaknesses, you can make choices that align with your goals. Lavallo and Sibony's research has shown that decision-makers like to work in specific ways and they should understand their tendencies to keep them from undermining their intent. Making sound choices ultimately will help you build a successful business.

The research is still in its early stages. However, through their study, they have concluded that decision-making styles fall into six pairs of opposite preferences.

Table 5. Decision-Making Style Preferences[3]	
Ad hoc	Process
Action	Caution
Gathers Information Narrowly	Gathers Information Widely
Believes Corporate Interests Prevail	Believes Personal Interests Prevail
Likes Continuity	Likes Change
Storytelling	Facts

If you were to choose one from each pair of the above preferences, which would you prefer? The strength of this research is it acknowledges that everyone has their own ways they prefer to work. Knowing your preferences will help you in your relationships with other people and in making good choices. Moreover, understanding how others make decisions can help you have more knowledge of their process and thus to collaborate better.

What follows is a synopsis of the five styles of decision makers in more detail.

Visionary

The visionary decision maker is, according to Erik Sherman, "a champion of radical change with a natural gift for leading people through turbulent times."[4] Such people like change, gather information relatively narrowly, and are strongly biased toward action. However, visionaries sometimes make decisions without giving them much thought.

A visionary leader needs to take the time to study the business without rushing into an option. Talking with many franchisees will assist in the process and help you make an informed decision. Discuss your options with family and mentors and people who can add unbiased insight. A visionary may be more likely to fall victim to "love at first sight" without taking the time to get to know a franchise's business culture, the nature of the day-to-day work, and if the business is a good fit for their personal profile. From time to time, I hear of someone who purchased a franchise and within a few months closed the business. Perhaps they were visionaries that rushed into the wrong decision?

Guardian

According to Sherman, a guardian is a "model of fairness who preserves the health, balance, and values of the organization."[5] Such people have sound decision-making processes, try to make fact-based choices, and plan carefully. They are moderately cautious and gather information relatively widely. The guardian can be too cautious and slow-moving during a crisis when change is needed expeditiously.

The guardian may be overly cautious and may overanalyze the information needed to make a decision. Guardians need to be encouraged to move forward to make a change. The guardians are potential business owners that have difficulty taking the last step in making a decision. They probably will never make the changeover, they will look at all the information, remain overly cautious, and without the push of a spouse, partner, mentor, or some other means, they move forward with reluctance, if at all.

If you're a Guardian, get your facts, and seek help committing to a decision.

Motivator

Sherman explains that "Motivators are excellent choices for change. They are charismatic, can convince people of the need for action, and build alignment among parts of the company."[6] However, motivators are good at telling stories and sometimes believe the story to be true even if there is evidence to prove otherwise.

Motivators often do not gather enough information before making a decision. A good spreadsheet is particularly important for a motivator so they can put information about their business choices in one area, gather the relevant facts, and use the information to make a decision. A motivator, like the visionary, may make a quick decision while overlooking the facts. They may be the person who says that a particular business is good because they always have a line of cars in the drive-thru, or they may conclude that a particular business activity is terrible because their friend had a bad experience. If you're a motivator, learn to take the time to look at the facts and carefully evaluate the information before giving up on an option or rushing into an alternative.

Flexible

Flexible leaders are more versatile than other types of leaders. Sherman says they are, "comfortable with uncertainty, open minded in adapting to circumstances, and willing to involve a variety of people in the decision making."[7] They mildly lean to informal approaches rather than formal processes and are relatively cautious.

The flexible leader is very versatile and does well to include others in their decisions. However, they often fall into analysis paralysis due to analyzing too much information. Setting deadlines and adhering to them will help the flexible decision maker move forward. When looking at franchise and business options, set deadlines for final decisions. As Benjamin Franklin said, "Time is money."

Catalyst

In Erik Sherman's words, "The catalyst is an excellent person to lead the work of groups, whether making decisions or implementing them."[8] Catalysts are balanced; they prefer action to caution and typically tend toward broadly gathering information. The catalyst doesn't lean too much one way or the other. If you are a catalyst, you may need to create a different approach to making costly decisions to avoid poor results. Involving others in the decision is recommended for the catalyst.

Your decision-making style

Which of the above decision-making styles best describes your decision-making style? Do you feel you lean toward one decision-making style more than the others, or are you in the middle of the road like a catalyst? The McKinsey[9] website provides graphs of the decision-making styles at their site which you may find useful for further understanding your style.

Being aware of the type of decision maker you are will go a long way to helping you make thoughtful, useful decisions. Beware of the pitfalls of your particular style and find ways to prevent yourself from stepping into them.

BUILDING DECISION-MAKING SKILLS

The strongest principle of growth lies in human choice.
—George Eliot

Decision making is such an essential skill that there are many studies on how successful people make decisions. Building key decision-making skills is one of the foundations of personal and business success. Highly successful people often attribute their success to making the right decisions at the right time. Determining the outcomes desired and the timeliness of the decision are relevant factors in making decisions.

We all make thousands of decisions every day. These decisions have consequences that result in positive or negative outcomes. Acquiring the skills to make good choices is paramount to living a productive life.

Essential Skills

Decision-making skills help us make informed, effective decisions. *DecisionInnovation.com* has an extensive website with information on making sound decisions. Their *decision-making model*[10] helps identify knowledge and abilities essential to making wise choices, and they may not all be what you'd expect.

Following are the skills they recommend and how they relate to buying a business or franchise.

- A decision-making process that provides a consistent set of steps leading to a decision. *Follow our 6-step method to choosing a franchise or business.*

- Imagination and visualization of possible future consequences of alternative solutions. *Imagine what life will be like in your next business—what other options do you have as alternatives?*

- Information, data gathering, and observation methods that enable evaluation of solution. *See Decision-making steps 4 and 5.*

- Assessment of risk and uncertainty and application of probabilistic analysis to the likelihood of outcomes. *Avoid unnecessary risk.* Don't take on more debt than you can financially handle. You may want to put off buying a new car until your business is showing a good return on investment. Overextending yourself at this time will only add stress. *How risk averse are you? Have you assessed the business with factual analysis?*

- Develop coping strategies that help manage emotion and perception issues while increasing objectivity in stressful decision situations. *Realize when you are becoming emotional about your options and be aware of the fear factor. See Step Two.*

- Self-discipline and leadership skills that inspire and motivate commitment and action for a chosen solution. *Commit yourself to the process and drive yourself to complete it. See Step Two, Strategy Nine.*

- Time and task management needed for successful decision implementation. *Set time and task-related goals and hold yourself accountable for completing tasks on time. See Step Four, Stage two.*

A PROVEN DECISION-MAKING PROCESS

Making good decisions is a crucial skill at every level.
—Peter Drucker

When making an important decision, it is wise to follow a proven decision-making process. We are not naturally born decision makers—we rather develop a thought process over time and through experience. Often the wrong decisions teach us what not to do rather than what to do. Using a step-by-step process will help you make more deliberate, effective decisions. A proven method is especially, useful for life-changing decisions such as starting a business.

The University of Massachusetts[11] outlines a seven-step process for decision-making—and I have added the correlating steps in this book.

1. **Identify the decision.** Clearly define the decision you need to make. What is your goal? What is the purpose of this goal? Why do you want to make this change? (Step 1)

2. **Gather information.** Gather all necessary materials to make an informed decision. Talk with people who have professional experience in the area of your goal. Conduct research into the outcomes desired. (Step 3)

3. **Identify the alternatives.** What alternatives do you have? List all possible and desirable options. When choosing a franchise or business, you have many choices. (Step 3)

4. **Weigh the evidence.** Imagine what it would be like to carry out your choices. Whom will your choices affect? How will your decision affect you? Which options carry more emotional and intrinsic value? Identify which opportunities have the most potential to meet your goals. Rank them in order of preference. (Steps 3 and 4)

5. **Choose among the alternatives.** Make a choice. Most likely your choice will be the first of your preferences in Step 4 (Explore your options). Kescia Gray explains, "Understanding that this step can cause some people a lot of anxiety is important because this is where you have to trust your instincts. Although you may still be slightly indecisive about your final decision, you have to take into account how this makes you feel."[12]

6. **Take action.** Take action on your choice—begin to implement it now. (Steps 4 and 5)

7. **Review the decision and its consequences.** Contemplate the results of your choice and if it met the need in #1. Realize it may take some time for your goal to come to fruition. (Step 4 and 6)

The seven steps in the decision-making process give you a chance to analyze your decision using a methodical approach rather than a more emotional approach.

Table 6. Seven Step Decision Making Process

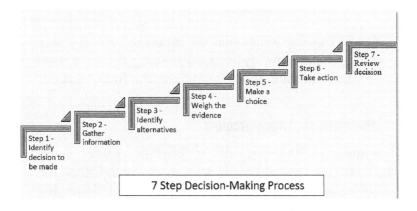

7 Step Decision-Making Process

DECISION-MAKING PITFALLS

Kescia D. Gray writes that while taking a step-by-step process helps simplify decision-making, there are some pitfalls to beware of before making the final decision.

Identifying the wrong problem

Sometimes the problem is obvious. Other times identifying the problem is not so straightforward. Sometimes people confuse the process of narrowing their franchise options with the process of investigating a franchise, however, *examining the individual franchise is more important than looking at alternatives.*

Only looking at one source

As I have mentioned before, when considering the significance of purchasing a given franchise, you must be open to obtaining information from more than one source. Many times potential franchise owners decide they want one particular franchise and only that one will do. If they work solely with the one franchise, they're making the salesperson's job quite easy and he or she will be happy to oblige by giving you the information you want, rather than the information you need to make an informed choice.

Too Many Sources

Looking at a variety of sources for information is good. However, too much information can cause information overload. When working with potential franchisees, I narrow their options to two or three. Any more than that and they become confused. It's like when a child tries to choose candy at the grocery store: there are so many choices she doesn't know what to do. I've worked with potential franchisees who have looked at twenty or thirty different franchises (on their own, never on my advice!). They wound up with information overload, and in the end, most could not make a choice.

Unrealistic projections

Everyone wants to make a million dollars the first year in business. However, that is unrealistic for most people. Make realistic projections based on facts and realize there is the possibility your outcomes will be less than estimated due to unforeseen circumstances. Unfortunately, some people overestimate their time to ROI (return on investment) and underestimate their capital requirements. Allowing a cushion in your savings for investment capital will go a long way in alleviating stress.

TIMING

The best time to plant a tree was 20 years ago. The second best time is now.

—Chinese proverb

It's important to understand how the timing of a decision affects your outcomes—particularly when starting a business or franchise. The cost of inaction can lead to the loss of revenues, territories, lease options, and financial rewards. When I owned a retail gift shop, I needed to have my holiday items purchased by June or July to have them in time for the Christmas season. If I waited too long, I would not receive the inventory, and I would miss out on some fantastic sales. Seasonal businesses all run this way. If you are opening a landscaping company, for instance, you will want to open before the mowing season begins.

Rushing into a decision such as starting a business or buying a franchise should not be taken lightly. However, there are times when expediency is your best friend. If you have recently been laid-off or displaced, the sooner you make your decision, the better. Consider the opportunity cost of waiting. Each day, week, month, and year you go without opening your business is time you are unable to build the actual business.

Conquer only one important decision at a time

There are times when it may be best to wait. Making too many life changes at one time only creates stress and confusion. For example: buying a house, moving, or getting married while starting your business makes it hard to focus and stay on track.

Set deadlines to maintain timeliness

Once you have decided that you are going to buy a franchise or start a business, it is best to put a timeline on your opening. Using a step-by-step process will help you stay on task. Break it into doable parts. Give yourself deadlines for each step. Do not try to take on too much at one time. This decision is a significant life choice, so making it in haste is not advised; however, not providing yourself with a deadline is like planning to procrastinate. Without a deadline, there is a danger of running into analysis paralysis, information bias, procrastination, and complacency. Deadlines for each step will help you stay on task.

Delay limits options

If you delay your decision to open a franchise, your options become limited, and you may be left with fewer alternatives. It's possible the territory may sell out, or the ideal location may be leased to someone else. Your franchise developer may cease to think of you as a good prospect if you delay your decision for an extended period. Franchises want leaders who can make sound, timely decisions.

Don't wait for the perfect time

If you are thinking, "now is not the time to start a business," I've got important news for you: *There is never a perfect time to get started.* Hundreds if not thousands of businesses have been started during the worst of times and thrived. The Kauffman Foundation sponsored a 2009 study that found more than half of the companies on the 2009 Fortune 500 list launched during a recession or bear market. Examples include:

- John D. Rockefeller invested in an oil refinery in 1863 during the Civil War.

- General Electric started in 1890 during a global economic recession.

- IBM started in 1896 during a U.S. economic slump.

- Walt Disney Productions reincorporated in 1929 right in the middle of the depression.

- Microsoft was founded in 1975 during a time of rising stagflation.[13]

These examples prove that there is no "perfect" time to go out on your own. If your dream is to own your own business and you have the skills and have prepared for your venture, the best time is now. Do not put off till tomorrow what you can do today. Tomorrow may never come.

PROCRASTINATION IS COSTLY

Procrastinating comes at a price. The longer you delay, the longer it will be before you start seeing a return on your investment. Every day you put off making a choice is one more day till you can open your business and begin to reap the rewards. Sometimes people put off their decision because they feel they may be more prepared if they delay. However, it can be like an artist when they paint a picture or an author working on a story; it will never be complete or good enough. However, there comes a time when they have to decide to put it out in the world.

Push yourself to move forward and open the doors to your dreams.

According to the Business Dictionary, *opportunity cost* is defined as "an alternative given up when a decision is made. A benefit, profit, or value of something that must be given up to acquire or achieve something else".[14] When trying to make a decision, you need to weigh the opportunity versus the alternative. What are you giving up in order to attain another alternative? Putting off a decision to start a business until 'the time is right' has an opportunity cost. There is also the cost of continuing on your current path and not creating your destiny.

Change does not come automatically. There is an action that needs to take place. People who are looking to open a business want to change their situation. Yet, they procrastinate for various reasons and sometimes they never realize their potential. If running your own business is your dream, you must motivate yourself to move forward and see your quest come to fruition. Committing to make a change is paramount for your dreams to come true.

Timeliness

That said, there is a kind of art to timeliness, or waiting just long enough but not too long. Keith TenBrook of *Decision Innovation.com* helps us understand the importance of timing:

The image below helps visualize the competing forces at work when trying to find the best time to reach a decision.

Too little time and the decision is made without knowledge that could have enabled a more informed choice, generally reducing risk. Too much time and the benefits from the alternative solutions are delayed, or in the case of a problem, losses, or pain continue to increase.[15]

Table 7. Best Time to Decide

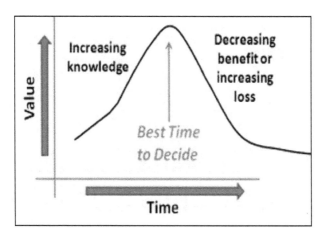

Decision Innovation.com

If you decide too early, you may rush into a decision and choose a franchise that is not suitable for your goals or lifestyle. There are some who get excited about a franchise just because someone else is buying it (operating on the herd instinct) and some who buy the newest brand and later regret their hasty decision.

If you are considering a seasonal business, what is the best time of year to grow revenues? Will you be queued up at the beginning of the season? If you wait to start at the end of the season, are you prepared for a few lean months before seeing a return on your investment?

TOOLS AND RESOURCES FOR EFFECTIVE DECISION MAKING

There are many tools and resources to read and use to assist with effective decision making. Writing your thoughts down in a constructive way is helpful in creating your vision.

A Decision-Making Worksheet

Creating and filling out a worksheet can be a valuable tool in your toolbox. Follow the tasks below to create a spreadsheet or worksheet to help you deliberate your choices.

Task 1 — Be accountable

Procrastination kills opportunities. What decisions regarding owning a business or franchise have you been putting off? List three:

1.
2.
3.

Task 2 — Prepare yourself

Are you feeling anxious about making the decision? Use the research from previous steps to boost your confidence. Pick one of the problems from the previous step. List the information you need to move forward and the experts and colleagues who can offer advice.

Info Needed:

People Needed:

Task 3 — Reflect

Once you've completed the first two steps, reflect upon where that knowledge takes you. What insights did you gain? Did you discover things below the surface? List your realizations:
1.
2.
3.

Task 4 — Establish your action plan

What do you need to do before you take action? Should you meet with key stakeholders? Consult with an expert? List your next moves and give yourself a deadline to make them.

Action 1:   Deadline:
Action 2:   Deadline:
Action 3:   Deadline:

Go through that four-step process, and your decisions will look much more attainable.

Make the process easier by acting immediately. Use your knowledge; don't put off the decision. Be confident and do not look back—move onward!

Remind yourself of the payoff. Remember why you are looking for a business and your dream.

Keep away from people who try to belittle your ambitions. Small people always do that, but the really great make you feel that you, too, can become great.
                              —Mark Twain

DECISION ANALYSIS TOOLS

The sign of intelligent people is the ability to control their emotions by the application of reason.
—Marya Mannes

Many decision-making techniques can help you with your outcomes and effectiveness. Methods that will assist with your business finding process are varied. Choose the one that seems most comfortable for you to implement.

Pro/Con Table

A pro/con table would be useful at the beginning of your process when trying to decide to leave your job to start a business. You can list pros and cons on a chart for each of your options. You can even use a rating scale to assist in your choice.

Table 8. Pros vs. Cons Chart			
PROS	Rating 1-5	CONS	Rating 1-5
Total		Total	

Decision Matrix

A simple decision matrix is a spreadsheet with criteria for evaluation of your franchise options. Decide the criteria that are most important to you in your business. You may want to ask your franchise consultant about criteria that are important for you to consider adding to this list. Then score your franchise options by how well they meet your requirements. Give them a number from 0 to 5, with 0 being lowest and 5 being highest, for each element. Add your total scores to determine the alternative with the highest number of criteria met. A decision matrix is a great option when you are having difficulty deciding between any two or three options—for example, when buying a home or a new car.

Table 9. Decision Matrix (example)
List criteria you want in your business

Criteria (Examples)	Option #1 Rate 0-5	Option #2 Rate 0-5	Option #3 Rate 0-5
Flexible Hours			
Multiple units			
Mobile units			
Territory location			
Comfort with investment level			
Totals			

Paired Comparison Analysis

Using paired comparison is a good option when you have your choices narrowed down to two. Important criteria of the two options are compared and analyzed. After listing your criteria, complete the data in the chart for each option. Then you can highlight a preferable option and compare information. The option with the most highlighted items would appear to be the winner.

Table 10. Paired-Comparison Chart (examples)

Criteria Examples	Option #1	Option #2
Time in business	10 years	20 years
Number of franchises	250	100
Investment level	$150,000	$250,000
Size of territory	5,000 businesses	10,000 businesses

These decision analysis tools are beneficial when trying to make a monumental decision such as buying a business, buying a home, or even changing careers. When you can put a visual to the criteria, you will gain clarity to your choice. Use these tools to guide you in your choice, then choose the one that seems like the best fit.

> *Nothing is more difficult, and therefore more precious, than being able to decide.*
> —Napoleon Bonaparte

For more information on decision-making skills, check out the book *Smart Choices: A Practical Guide to Making Better Decisions* by John Hammond, Ralph Keeney, and Howard Raiffa, published in 1999 it is a great resource for making better decisions.

Seth Godin is one of my most admired writers, a marketing guru, and business educator. He writes a blog every single day and has done so for more than 15 years! This blog from August 2018 about making difficult decisions is relevant to this section.

Difficult decisions

These are the decisions that are forced on us, the ones that feel unfair, and the ones where there are no seemingly good outcomes.

How to proceed?

1. Acknowledge that it sucks. That you'd rather not be in this situation. That it's not what you hoped for. You can return to this step as often as you like, but don't permit it to have anything to do with the other steps in the process.
2. Consider the sunk costs. The things you did to get to this point, the hard work and investments you made to have what you had until recently. Now, *ignore them*. They're sunk. They have no connection to the decision you need to make.
3. Outline your options. None of them are as happy as you'd hope. None are perfect. All involve a measure of discomfort. That's okay, because that's what's on offer. Write them out.

Now, consider each option based on the future, not the past. Ignoring the sunk costs, ignoring what you deserve, which of these options offers you the happiest series of future days, weeks and months? Choose that one. Don't look back. Go.[16]

Build your own dreams, or someone else will hire you to build theirs.

—Farrah Gray

STEP SIX

REALITIES OF RUNNING A BUSINESS

Many people believe that when their business opens, they will become instantly rich, will hire people to do all their work, and will ride off into the sunset in a new Mercedes. You need to know, if you don't already, that this is not the way it really is. Once you open your business, there is a great deal of serious work to do. In this section, we look at approaches to help you mentally prepare for operating your business.

YOU WILL NEED TO WORK HARD

Back in 2012, when President Obama said, "If you've got a business, you didn't build that,"[1] I took it as a personal insult to hard-working small business owners everywhere. He may have been talking about the importance of civic infrastructure, however, in the process, he diminished the hard work of individuals. I still haven't forgotten it.

Let me explain.

The Family Business

I grew up surrounded by our family business. My dad grew up on a farm and worked hard all his life. Before my parents were married, my dad and his three brothers built my parents' home (yes, they *built* that). After the first house, the brothers proceeded to construct homes for each other until they each had a home for their families. Due to the booming population after

World War II, new homes were in demand and the brothers opened a business as homebuilders.

They bought some land in town and proceeded to build homes one street at a time. Their business grew; and before long they were building commercial buildings, banks, shopping centers, churches, nursing homes, stores, and doctors' offices. That is why, when we are driving in the area, we often point out buildings that the brothers built (and we say, "Hey, they built that!").

Building a Business is Hard Work

Little did I know what went into building my fathers' business. My father worked *long* hours. He was in charge of running the business side of things, coordinating the supplies, talking with customers, making sure they complied with permits, licensing, and building codes. I very rarely heard him complain. I believe he loved his work, seeing the progress, taking an open space and building homes, making his customers happy, and growing the business.

The American Dream

My dad had a very keen mind. He had a high school education, and he was very successful. He lived the American dream. Our family lived the American dream. My father instilled in me the American dream—you can start from nothing and build a successful business. Nowhere else in the world do you have the opportunities that you do in the U.S.A.

Even though my father died at a young age, I marvel at what he accomplished in his short life. I miss him, his wit, and his wisdom; so much of what I have been able to do I owe to what he taught me.

Small Business is Empowering

This is why I like to help people find a business that is a good fit for them. I have experienced the feeling of success through business ownership; I saw it with my father every day, the sense of accomplishment, building something, hard work paying off, using your skills and mind to grow a business. In my own life, I have owned several small businesses, and the feeling of empowerment that comes from owning a business is very gratifying.

EVERY DAY WILL BE DIFFERENT

No one enjoys their job all of the time—even if it's their own business. Be prepared for the highs and lows, for thrilling days and discouraging days. It takes time to build a business, and you will get a lot of "no's" in the beginning. It's like a game of chance: the more chances you take, the better your odds. More "no's" means you are getting closer to a "yes." As you work your way through the myriad decisions and tasks, you can tweak your methods and processes by tracking sales and marketing data and using that information to improve. One big break or a lot of small sales can make your year. A franchise takes a lot of the decision-making off your back since they have already worked out many of the minor decisions through their processes.

If you are the type of person who likes variety in your work, owning a business may be right for you, as you will be sure to have a variety of responsibilities and tasks. Bear in mind the worst that can happen along with the best. Be prepared with a scenario to cover any obstacle you may encounter. Ask current franchisees what they would list as some problematic situations they have faced. Also, ask them what they find most rewarding to the business.

Learn to enjoy the discomfort of change.

Zach Obront writes, "Far too many of our problems—whether in business, relationships or day-to-day life—come from clinging to the past. By enjoying the discomfort of change, we open ourselves up to see things from a new perspective, and to be happier while doing it."[2]

The following table lists a few benefits and challenges of any business. Add your own for your specific industry or any others that come to mind.

Table 11. Benefits and challenges of business ownership

Benefits	Challenges
✓ Giving back to the community. ✓ Getting to know your customers. ✓ Meeting other business owners and building relationships with them. ✓ Flexible hours (depending upon the business). ✓ Sales beyond all expectations. ✓ Positive customers who talk about how you helped them. ✓ The feeling of accomplishment when you complete a challenging project. ✓ Learning new skills. ✓ Employees who excel in their positions. ✓ Days when everything seems to go right. ✓ Orders come in correctly and on time. ✓ Add your own for the industry.	✓ Customers that are not satisfied and complain no matter what you do. ✓ Working all hours to complete a particular project. ✓ The learning curve is taxing. ✓ Employees who have no motivation. ✓ Bills are more than you take in for sales (cash flow). ✓ Work seems like it's never ending. ✓ Days when everything seems to go wrong. ✓ Problems with technology and equipment. ✓ Orders are damaged, late or incorrect. ✓ Bad reviews on social media. ✓ Add your own for the industry.

Preparation is key to your success. The most *difficult obstacles occur with people, processes, communication, and timing.* Keep these in mind when planning your business.

LESSONS LEARNED THROUGH BUSINESS OWNERSHIP

Entrepreneurs work 80 hours a week so they can avoid working 40 hours a week for someone else.
—Lori Greiner

When I started my first retail store, I learned many truths about owning a business versus working for someone else. Following is a list of realities about being in business for yourself.

Lesson #1: Business does not sleep.

I never took a day off in my twenties. Not one.
—Bill Gates

Even though my first business was a gift shop with limited hours, I was working my business most of my waking hours. It's not like you can leave your business behind when you leave the building. I was always thinking of ways to improve the business or about the tasks that needed to be taken care of the next day or week. There may be calls you need to make while at home, emails to answer, orders to fill, networking events to attend, and bookkeeping to complete. Running that shop and owning a business was all-consuming. Moreover, it was also a fantastic learning experience, and I enjoyed it very much.

I especially enjoyed the people I met and the customers that became friends. Owning a business takes time. Furthermore, it is very empowering when you get to make the decisions. Be sure to talk with your family about the amount of time you will need to put into the business in the beginning. The payoff can be huge, and, it will take time and patience to bear the fruit of your labors.

Lesson #2: Working 9–5 holds you back from getting rich

> *Entrepreneurship is living a few years of your life like most people won't, so you can spend the rest of your life like most people can't.*
> —Unknown

If you study successful people who started from nothing and are now millionaires or billionaires, you will find long hours, devotion and determination are keys to success.

Grant Cardone is a self-made millionaire, and he says people need to work more hours to reach the seven-figure status. Writing in Medium, Cardone says, "Most people work 9 to 5. I work 95 hours (per week).

If you ever want to be a millionaire, you need to stop doing the 9 to 5 and start doing 95."[3] Other self-made millionaires say working a 9 to 5 job holds people back. "Steve Siebold, who spent 25 years studying wealthy individuals for his book *How Rich People Think*, notes that there is a critical difference in how the wealthy and everyone else choose to get paid. Average people prefer wages based on time—an hourly rate, for example—while the rich are typically self-employed and get paid based on results."[4]

Individuals who stay in a job with a low to moderate income, find it's impossible to get ahead. To live a life of abundance, you need to get out of a mediocre career, into a business where you have no limits. Making a plan, believe in yourself, and taking action is how you can attain financial success. When you work a salary position, it does not matter how many hours you work, you typically make the same amount of money, or your salary can only go so high. When you own your own business, there are infinite possibilities.

Cardone writes, "There's no shortage of money. There is a shortage of people doing 95 hours each week."[5]

I doubt I'll ever go back to corporate work. Once you see the light, there is no turning back.

—Magnus Jepson

Lesson #3: Never go back to the corporate world

Many people think that if you own a business, you must be rich. You may be rich in blessings, however, blessings do not pay the bills. Some people are lucky enough to strike it rich right away. However, those people are few and far between. It takes time to build a business. You should be prepared to go a year or even two without income. Having a spouse or partner who is still working and can pay household expenses is the best way to get through the first few challenging months before you see a return on your investment. With a franchise, it will be easier to predict your time to positive cash flow than if you start from scratch because of the franchises track record and information you receive during your diligence process.

Steven Boehle of CoBound Marketing, writes, "In the very beginning of my first business, my business partner and I scraped by. Working out of my garage, eating Ramen noodles, and living like college kids again. Any additional income went back to the business, trying to get it to grow. I have talked to many business owners from all over that have sold their homes and moved back to their parents' home to save cash. Definitely, something you hope not to happen."[6]

Boehle talks about the long-term goals of owning a business:

> *If you think that starting your business is going to generate tons of cash right off the bat, you're crazy and probably starting your company for the wrong reason. Profit is a long-term goal, but the benefit can be tremendous and make all the hard work worth it.[7]*

Luxuries like a vacation, new vehicles, and dinners out often are put on the back-burner for months or years when starting a business. I always found the journey the most motivating aspect of growing my business. Joshua Harris, founder of Quantum Jump Consulting advises you learn to live within your means:

I didn't take a vacation for years until I got my business to a consistent point that my lifestyle cannot even make a dent in it. If you're living well within your means and investing in education and skills, one day you'll wake up with more than enough to afford the things you want, and have the cash reserves.[8]

Once you have made it through the first few difficult months till you can start seeing a payback, you will still need to continue to direct your efforts to grow the business. You will want to put money back into the company for future needs. Realize you are building equity for the day when it comes time to sell the business or pass it on to your family. Equity in the business is money in the bank.

Lesson #4: Sales is vital to success

Keep your sales pipeline full by prospecting continuously. Always have more people to see than you have time to see them.

—Brian Tracy

Do you have negative connotations of pushy salespeople? Do you dread selling? Realize right now: if you own a business, you will always be selling. It may be consultative selling, online selling, or direct sales. However, it is still selling. If you are an experienced sales professional, you have an advantage. If not, you can learn through networking with others and by taking courses that will help you build this valuable skill.

"Sandler Training"[9] is one of many companies that offers an excellent system for training sales professionals through local franchisees. You may want to check out their training or another sales training option.

There are thousands of books on sales you might find helpful. To save time, you can download recorded books and listen to them while traveling, walking, or doing other work. I enjoy listening to books because they are motivating and educational while saving time.

Mark Cuban wrote a blog post titled *A Couple of My Rules for Startups* where he said, "Sales Cures All. Know how your company will make money and how you will actually make sales."[10] Focusing on sales pays off in big ways. There is a myriad of other things that can get in the way. Nevertheless, sales must be at the top of your list.

Matt Roberge writes sales are not simple yet, sales is the lifeblood of a business:

> *If you own a small business, you are in sales. Period. If you can't sell, you are dead. Many entrepreneurs underestimate the importance and difficulty of sales. They just think that obviously, someone will want to buy their stuff.*[11]

Prospecting for business is crucial in the first few months when you need to build your image and product recognition. You can learn how to be an effective salesperson. There are plenty of resources available. With determination and persistence along with a competitive spirit, you can learn how to sell. Taking action will pay off in ways you never expected. Remember: No sales = no profit = no pay.

To me, job titles don't matter. Everyone is in sales.
It's the only way we stay in business.

—Harvey Mackay

Lesson #5: A small business owner must be a Jack-of-all-trades

When you start your business, you are the boss. You should know how to do all of the daily tasks, even if you have employees. Many people start as a sole proprietor, so they are taking care of all the day-to-day tasks. Depending upon the type of business, the responsibilities will include bookkeeping, marketing, advertising, website, and computer maintenance, sales, networking, scheduling, quoting, consulting, ordering, banking, cleaning, producing, managing, hiring employees, shipping and receiving, customer service, and so forth. There will be tasks you do not like and tasks you love to do, and there will be tasks you do not get done.

Are you organized and a good planner? Unfortunately, poor planning contributes to many business failures. You will need to keep track of inventory, schedules, marketing, and finances. Staying organized in these areas will help avoid challenges.

If you are struggling with specific tasks, do not be afraid to hire an expert who can get the work done faster and with more accuracy. There are thousands of freelancers ready to help with marketing, designing logos, website updates, human resources, and bookkeeping. Garenne Bigby writes a blog about the *Top 25 websites for freelancers.*[12] The list includes Upwork, Fiverr, and 99designs, with a brief description of each.

This list is useful and very interesting to read if you're in the market for a freelancer.

A Jack-of-all-trades makes a good entrepreneur because they know how to look at the big picture from their full breadth of experiences. Consider the likes of Leonardo DaVinci and Ben Franklin who are famous for their various inventions and artistry. If you're always learning new things, maybe you'll be the next Leonardo of franchising!

> *So often people are working hard at the wrong thing. Working on the right thing is probably more important than working hard.*
> —Caterina Fake

Lesson #6: Mistakes are inevitable

There will be times when you make mistakes. Learn from your mistakes and move on. Forgot to order merchandise? Try another brand and add a reminder to your calendar for next time. There are thousands of tasks you will need to do and keep track of when you own a business. Learning to organize yourself, so you do not forget something will come with experience— and quickly; probably within the first few months. Owning a franchise will give you a pathway for your organization because of the written instructions.

Lesson #7: Everyday will not be "peaches and cream"

Realize that every day will not be exactly as you imagine and mentally prepare for setbacks. Look on them as challenges and believe that you have the tools to get through whatever it is. You will be stronger for it. Your belief in yourself and those around you will build confidence, in turn, your confidence will grow. Inevitably, surprises will come up and flexibility will be necessary.

Lesson #8: Focus on building the business

Stay focused on the crucial tasks. It's easy to get lost in the small things, regardless, staying focused on getting customers will be more important than spending time reading emails. As soon as possible, hire someone to do mundane tasks so you can put your energy into growing the business. Though it may feel like you're neglecting less important parts of the business, increasing customers will pay off in significant ways later when your business begins to grow organically.

Hiring a freelancer or virtual assistant may cost more than if you do it yourself, but consider the cost of taking your time away from prospecting for sales. Maximize your transferable skills and focus on the big picture, which is growing the business and getting new customers. Leave tasks that are challenging for you to others who have more expertise.

Concentrate on your business, so you do not fall off track and lose your momentum. Say *no* to activities that will distract you from your laser focus.

Lesson #9: Become a lifelong learner

What sculpture is to a block of marble, education is to the soul.

—Joseph Addison

Embrace learning opportunities as much as your time allows. Continually learning in this constantly changing technology environment is paramount to success. Reading books by other entrepreneurs is inspiring and motivating and gives you the opportunity to learn how others became successful. If you search for lists of good business books or good sales books, you will find quite a few lists. Hubspot has a blog by Aja Frost listing "The 23 Most Highly-Rated Sales Books of All Time"[13] which might be worth a look for you. You may also want to check and read the reviews on Amazon.

I often listen to Audible[14] books while traveling in the car or working in the office. Recorded books are a great way to get your reading in while you are doing something else. Libraries are an excellent resource for recorded books, eBooks, and business publications all at no cost to you.

The Small Business Administration provides many free services and information for those who want to start a business. The SBA is a great place to seek answers to your business questions. Their website is solely focused on small business and helping businesses get started. They offer webinars and articles on various topics related to business.

Conferences can be another source of learning and motivation, be careful only to attend meetings benefitting your business with tools and strategies you can use right away. I once met a woman who was spending all her money attending conferences and did not have enough time to build her business or enough money to invest in marketing. Do attend your annual franchise conference as it is essential to building relationships with the franchisor and franchisees while learning about new products and processes.

Do not be afraid to admit what you do not know. If you are not sure of something, ask or find out the answer. No one knows everything so admit what you do not know and allow an expert to help you.

Lesson #10: Learning to network will help you and your business grow

When you own a business, you have the opportunity to meet with people from various industries. Your network will grow, and you will enjoy learning about the challenges you share with other business owners. There are plenty of options for networking even if you live in a small town. Often new business owners are fearful about meeting new people. However, networking is an excellent tool for getting your business noticed and building relationships.

Attend networking groups and meetups in your area. These groups share referrals and information on best practices. If you cannot find such a group in your area, start one of your own. Starting a group will demonstrate your expertise and show you as a leader in the business community.

Of course, "networking" is a scary word for some people. Chris Borja, the founder of Become a Better Networker in Columbus, Ohio, talks about the fear of networking: "It's an understandable fear, because it's a skill that most people have never received any formal education or training in. In fact, networking goes against a belief that has been taught to us since early childhood ... 'Don't talk to strangers!'"

He offers this advice for getting past your fear of networking:

Getting past that fear is a worthwhile endeavor. Networking is one of the most beneficial and effective activities that can be done to accomplish one's business and personal goals. The best way to overcome any fears of networking, is to place the focus on others' needs rather than our own. If we can adopt the definition of networking as the collaboration between two or more people to share value and resources, it reduces the pressure for us to say the perfect thing, or give the perfect "pitch."

Here's a quick analogy to help understand the power of networking. Imagine playing the game of poker, but being allowed to exchange cards with the person next to you while the rest of the table plays by standard rules. It's clearly an advantage to share resources and improve each other's hand/situation. That's what happens when we learn to work together and collaborate, instead of compete.

Networking creates true win-win situations, and a serves as a long-term resource as true relationships and friendships are created.[15]

There are many opportunities to network with a wide variety of groups. Meetup[16] is a website with an app where you find groups of people with various interests in your geographical area. You can join these groups, with permission, and they have gatherings at different places. The interests vary from business to yoga. It's a fun way to meet new people and learn about topics that interest you.

Other options for networking are civic groups, such as Lions International[17], Rotary International[18], and Kiwanis International[19]. Your church may also offer opportunities for networking through classes or service organizations.

Some groups focus only on business referrals through networking. Two of these organizations are AmSpirit[20] and Business Networking International[21]. These membership organizations define the type of members in each group and allow only one from a category (such as banking, realtor, insurance, and finance). This method cuts down on competing businesses.

If you dread speaking in front of groups, you may want to join Toastmasters International[22]. At Toastmasters, members work on their speaking and leadership skills. This group provides extensive tools and a supportive community where members can hone speaking skills at their own pace with encouraging feedback.

Any time you meet with people, you are the face of your business. Keep in mind, talking about your business or "hard selling" during a gathering is not recommended. Building relationships are the goal, so when someone needs your service or product, they think of you.

MENTORS

As an entrepreneur, you will have the opportunity to work with mentors who will help guide your experiences. If a network is a series of professional relationships, a mentor is like a professional mother, uncle, or coach within your network.

Do not be afraid to ask for help from experienced business owners and mentors. Seek out programs that provide mentors to entrepreneurs. For example, SCORE (Service Corp of Retired Executives)[23] has an excellent *free* program of retired business executives that mentor business owners to help them get started and achieve success. Many business people enjoy helping others, so do not be afraid to ask. Utilizing this asset can prove priceless.

As a business owner, you will also have the chance to mentor others, which can be just as fulfilling as being mentored. Mentorship is another way to give back. Business people are very willing to share their success with others.

Obey the Golden Rule: *"Do unto others as you would have them do unto you."* Consider what you can do for others rather than what you can get from them. People can tell if you have their best interests at heart.

SURROUND YOURSELF WITH GREAT PEOPLE

This could be Lesson #11; however, it deserves a little more space. Running your own business is rewarding yet tough. Accordingly, surround yourself with people who are positive and will encourage you to be successful. One benefit of franchising is the built-in network of experienced management and franchisees you work with—all of whom will want you to achieve success. Holding a vision in common and sharing best practices are among the significant benefits of franchising. You do not need to reinvent the wheel; take advantage of the franchisee network.

Hire great employees

A great hire will lift your spirits, as well as your profits.

—Ray Zinn

Surrounding yourself with positive people in business is extremely important. Hiring super employees is even more critical. Look for people who are both motivated and motivating. Employees can make or break a company so do not take their employment lightly. Ideally, your team will fill in areas where you are weak so you can play to your strengths. Once you have hired good people, treat them well. Marcus Lemonis says that one of the biggest mistakes he sees among struggling entrepreneurs is that they do not value their employees enough. They do not take the time to train them properly.[24]

Keep it professional

I talked to a gentleman who had a great business model and was very successful until he hired employees. When I asked him what the problem was, he told me he had hired relatives and friends. These workers were not the right fit for the business and did not respect him as the owner. Hiring friends and family works out sometimes, however, be aware of the pitfalls. Firing a family member or your best friend is difficult and causes problems in your personal life as well.

Employees work for you, not the franchise

Typically, franchises have good hiring practices and will provide you with information regarding the type of employees to hire. However, it will be up to you to decide whom you want on your team. The employees work for you, not the franchise.

Write detailed job descriptions

Take the time to write detailed job descriptions of what you expect of the employee. Detailed job descriptions will help you address specific tasks and ask questions about those activities. Since you are starting small, your employees will probably need to have skills in more than one area. Be sure to address all areas where it is possible the employee will need to work. Finding out after you have hired someone that they refuse to drive the van or complete specific tasks is discouraging to everyone. Hiring the wrong employee can be very costly to any business, particularly a new small business.

Interviewing a potential employee

When holding the interview, allow the candidate to do most of the talking. Do what you can to make them feel comfortable. We all know that interviewing is stressful for most people. Pay attention to the candidate's attitude, especially, when they speak about specific types of job tasks or their past jobs. Bad-mouthing a former employer can be a red flag when hiring (how will they speak about you with other employees?). A positive attitude is essential to key employees, particularly if they will be working with customers and vendors.

Find out about their education and the kind of work they have done in the past. You're looking for a good match of skills with the tasks required for the position. Remember that you didn't have experience in the same industry as the franchise you now own—though you did have transferable skills!

Did the potential employee dress the part? I know a Human Resource Manager who talks about a young man interviewing for an engineering job. The interviewee had completed college and had been looking for a job for quite some time. He was offered an interview and showed up in an old tee shirt, torn jeans, and unkempt hair. He did not talk much at all and did not seem interested in the job. He may have had the skills for the job through his education, yet he did not dress the part, and he did not interview well. Consequently, he was not hired.

Unfortunately, these stories are told more and more often, as the interviewees seem to think an interview is 'come as you are.' Hold out for better than that.

Scoring candidates

To make it easier to hire objectively, score your interviewees by specific criteria. List your essential criteria on a table or spreadsheet and score your candidates on a scale of 1–10. Use your job description as a guide. Leave a box for notes you take while interviewing. Criteria vary by type of business, job description, and your expectations. Most companies would include objective criteria such as job experience, education, technical expertise, physical abilities (lifting boxes, standing on roofs, and other physical skills), and clerical skills. Subjective criteria could be attitude, written skills, appearance, cultural fit, customer service, and soft skills. Be sure to check references and add notes to your scoring based on the references' comments.

USING TOOLS TO HELP BUILD YOUR BUSINESS

We live in a time when computers have significantly increased the availability of tools to help build your business. Since sales are such an essential part of every business, there are many technological tools available, sometimes too many to choose from, so do some research to decide which tools make the most sense for your business.

Following is a list of tools you may want to take into consideration for your business. Your franchisor may have specific requirements for tools and software so be sure to ask before investing or spending time learning applications you will not use.

1. Social Media

According to studies, using social media to stay in touch with customers, keep up-to-date on new developments, and inform your audience will help boost your sales performance. Facebook, Twitter, LinkedIn, Instagram, and YouTube are the most widely used social selling methods today. Become familiar with these media and check out the types of ads and articles that are posted on a daily basis. Connecting with people through social media will help you build credibility and your network. Buffer and Hootsuite are a couple of options to increase your posting abilities. They offer scheduling options daily and several times a day to social media portals.

2. Customer Relationship Management (CRM)

Customer relationship management tools are the mainstay of seasoned sales professionals. They help organize everything from calendars, contact information, emails, inventories, ordering, bookkeeping, and more. Salesforce, Zoho, Pipedrive, and Microsoft Dynamics are a few of the CRMs to choose from. Most offer either a standard package or customization options for your business.

3. Apps to increase productivity

Staying organized and on top of your schedule is much easier with some of the productivity apps available. Sharing files and information with Dropbox and Google Drive makes it easier to transfer files through the cloud and work on documents from anywhere. Utilizing an online calendar is necessary for keeping appointments and staying on schedule. The calendar can be shared with others in the office so schedules can be easily coordinated. Reminders are handy for tracking important tasks and events. A voice recorder on your phone will help you remember what was said in important meetings and training (provided you use it). Calendly is one of several apps that customers can schedule an appointment or call with you—which helps avoid telephone tag. Check your app files for other options to increase productivity.

4. Email campaigns

Keeping in touch with customers, contacts, and potential customers is important, and you will make it much easier by using targeted email campaigns. Easily connect your email campaign application to your contact list and send out periodic newsletters, coupons, or special event notices. MailChimp and Zoho offer the ability to send email campaigns more manageable than sending snail mail or sending through your email system. They also will provide you statistics on who opened the email, unsubscribes, and when the emails were opened.

5. Understand your numbers with bookkeeping tools

A business owner needs to understand all the facets of the business—the sales, inventory, salaries, and how things move through the business. Staying on top of numbers is important, so you do not get behind and have an unwanted surprise down the road. Often your CRM will include bookkeeping programs; check it out. There are lots of classes and workshops available to help you understand the bookkeeping and accounting parts of your business. Take advantage of them and learn as much as you can about accounting as it truly is "the language of business."

YOU'RE THE BOSS — ENJOY IT!

The great use of life is to spend it for something that will outlast it.

—William James

Owning a business and creating your path is the American dream. My father worked long and hard day after day, yet he took time to spend with family. I have many happy memories of time spent with him and our family. I'm sure he had many stressful days, yet when he was home, he spent time with us. Do not lose sight of what is important to you.

Take time to care for yourself by exercising body and mind, eating right, and spending time doing things that will help you stay balanced. Working too hard causes stress and a lack of focus and can wear you thin. Caring for yourself will help you stay energized and innovative. A good adage is "work to live, don't live to work."

Nafise Nina Hodjat, founder and managing attorney of The SLS Firm, advises you to "be grateful, have fun and take care of others." Nafise grew up in an immigrant family and remembers her parents worked full-time jobs, yet they took time to enjoy family and have fun. She says to "enjoy the things money can't buy and give back to those in need. It makes the good days sweeter and the tough days easier".[25]

SET YOUR MIND TO IT

One way to be successful is to set your mind to your mission. Your mental attitude will determine how you respond to situations. Therefore, a positive mindset is imperative for success. Your mindset will make a huge difference in your determination to follow through and reach your goals. Developing a positive way of thinking involves changing the way you think. Following are characteristics of a positive mindset that will help you achieve your targets.

1. Inner Voice

Avoid negative, self-destructive thoughts. Your inner voice can be self-defeating or uplifting. Ignore the voices in your head that may tell you not to achieve your dreams. Maintain a focus on positive, motivating self-talk.

2. Purpose

Your purpose is the wish you plan to carry out. Setting your mind with determination and resolve to carry out your purpose is the catalyst that will set you on the path to your desired destination. Intend to do great work, focus on customer satisfaction and high levels of success. Follow through with your plans with enthusiasm.

3. Tenacity

Thomas Edison is credited with a famous adage about creativity and innovation: "Genius is 1 percent inspiration and 99 percent perspiration." Starting a new business is exciting, especially in the beginning. Having the grit and tenacity to push through the tough times is what makes a viable, successful business. Set your mind to push through challenges.

4. Plan

Have a strategic plan for how your business will run. "Fail to plan, and you plan to fail," as they say. Using SMART goals from Step Four will allow you to develop a strategy for a thriving business. Focus on your plans and strategies rather than obstacles.

5. Implementation

Planning and strategizing is one thing, yet implementing is even harder. Set your mind to follow through on your actions step-by-step, keep sight of your purpose, and be determined to carry through.

6. Review

After your business is up and running, periodically review your progress towards your goals. Then you can adjust where needed and make changes. Set your mind toward success and be determined to attain your purpose.

> *True happiness comes from the joy of deeds well done, the zest of creating things new.*
>
> —Antoine de Saint Exupery

THE POWER OF DREAMS

You may have picked up this book because of the desire to fulfill your dreams of owning your own business. Perhaps buying a franchise has conjured up visions of happiness and success. The human spirit is a powerful source of imagination, resourcefulness, and true grit. Recently, I read an article about the one thing that successful students possess to do well in school. It is not a high IQ, high ACT or SAT scores, or even economic factors. It is *grit*. It's the ability to grind through day after day, setting a goal and sticking with it, finishing what they start—whether it is a term paper or a year of college. I believe it is the same with those who start a business. Grit will get you far. Where there is a will, there is a way.

I caution everyone to be sure they have the right tools strategically and financially before starting their business or investing in a franchise. It takes a village to build a business, just as it takes a village to raise a child. Your business will be your baby, gather the right team, feed it the right ingredients, listen to the experts (everyone likes to give advice—too much advice can be detrimental and confusing), let it grow and in no time at all, it will flourish.

You have the potential for greatness and the power to do great things. Believe it!

Go confidently in the direction of your dreams! Live the life you've imagined.

—Henry David Thoreau

GLOSSARY OF COMMON FRANCHISE TERMS

Business format franchise: This type of franchise includes not only a product, service, and trademark, but also the complete method to conduct the business itself, such as the marketing plan and operations manuals.[1]

Business Opportunity: Legal definitions vary; in its simplest terms, a business opportunity is a packaged business investment that allows the buyer to begin a business. The Federal Trade Commission and 25 states regulate the concept.[2]

Business Opportunity Rule: requires business opportunity sellers to give prospective buyers specific information to help them evaluate a business opportunity, thus ensuring that the prospective purchasers have the information they need in order to assess the risks of buying a work-at-home program or any other business opportunity.[3]

Federal Trade Commission FTC: The FTC is a bipartisan federal agency with a unique dual mission to protect consumers and promote competition.[4]

Franchise Disclosure Document, FDD: The franchise disclosure document (FDD) is a legal disclosure document that must be given to individuals interested in buying a U.S. franchise as part of the pre-sale due diligence process. It contains information essential to potential franchisees about to make a significant investment. The format for the disclosure document which provides information about the franchisor and franchise system to the franchisee.[5]

Franchise: A franchise is a type of license that a party (franchisee) acquires to allow them to have access to a business's (the franchiser) proprietary knowledge, processes, and trademarks in order to allow the party to sell a product or provide a service under the business's name. In exchange for gaining the franchise, the franchisee usually pays the franchisor an initial start-up and annual licensing fees.[6]

Franchise agreement: A legal contract in which a well-established business consents to provide its brand, operational model and required support to another party for them to set up and run a similar business in exchange for a fee and some share of the income generated.[7] The franchise agreement lays out the details of what duties each party needs to perform and what compensation they can expect.

Franchise Rule: Gives prospective purchasers of franchises the material information they need in order to weigh the risks and benefits of such an investment. The rule requires franchisors to provide all potential franchisees with a disclosure document containing 23 specific items of information about the offered franchise, its officers, and other franchisees.[8] Also known as the FDD.

Franchisee: A franchisee is a small business owner that purchases the right to use an existing business's trademarks, associated brands, and other proprietary knowledge.[9]

Franchising: A method of business expansion characterized by a trademark license, payment of fees, and significant assistance and control.[10]

Franchisor: The person or company that grants the franchisee the right to do business under their trademark or trade name.[11]

Product distribution franchise: A franchise where the franchisee sells merely the franchisor's products without using the franchisor's method of conducting business.[12]

Royalty: The regular payment made by the franchisee to the franchisor, usually based on a percentage of the franchisee's gross sales.[13]

Small Business Administration SBA: The U.S. Small Business Administration (SBA) is an independent agency of the federal government to aid, counsel, assist and protect the interests of small business concerns, to preserve free competitive enterprise and to maintain and strengthen the overall economy of our nation.[14]

Trademark: The marks, brand name, and logo that identify a franchisor and is licensed to the franchisee.[15]

VetFran: An initiative of the IFA to provide access and opportunities in franchising to our Nation's Veterans and their Spouses.[16]

NOTES

Step One — Why?

1   Clifton, Jim. 2017. "The World's Broken Work-
    place." Gallop. 13 June. Accessed October 8, 2018.
    https://news.gallup.com/opinion/chairman/212045/
    world-broken-workplace.
2   Klein, Daniel B. 2018. "Survey Two Thirds of
    Americans Dream of Opening A Business."
    fool.com. 3 May. Accessed October 1, 2018.
    https://www.fool.com/careers/2018/05/02/
    survey-two-thirds-of-americans-drea
    m-of-opening-a.aspx.

Step Two — Confront the fear

1   Williamson, Marianne. 1993. *A Return to Love.* Large
    Print. Boston, MA: G. K. Hall & Co.
2   Tsaousides, Theo. 2018. "How to Conquer Fear
    of Failure." *Psychology Today.* 23 January. Accessed
    February 1, 2018. https://www.psychologytoday.

    com/us/blog/smashing-the-brainblocks/201801/
    how-conquer-fear-failure.

3   Fabella, Frederick. 2018. "Taking away the power of
    fear." *Articles Factory*. 5 January. Accessed February
    25, 2018. http://www.articlesfactory.com/articles/
    self-help/taking-away-the-power-of-fear.html.

4   Tsaousides, Theo. 2018. "How to Conquer Fear
    of Failure." *Psychology Today*. 23 January. Accessed
    February 1, 2018. https://www.psychologytoday.
    com/us/blog/smashing-the-brainblocks/201801/
    how-conquer-fear-failure.

5   Susan Weinschenk, PhD. 2018. "Have You
    Experienced the Imposter Syndrome?"
    Psychology Today. 19 March. Accessed March
    25, 2018. https://www.psychologytoday.
    com/us/blog/brain-wise/201803/
    have-you-experienced-the-imposter-syndrome.

6   Goodreads. 2018. "Thomas Edison Quotes."
    Goodreads.com. Accessed February 12, 2018. https://
    www.goodreads.com/author/quotes/3091287.
    Thomas_A_Edison.

7   Forleo, Marie. 2010. June. Accessed November
    30, 2017. https://www.marieforleo.com/2010/06/
    feel-failure-good/.

8   Tsaousides, Theo. 2015. "Is It Time to Face Your
    Biggest Fears?" *Psychology Today*. 5 November.
    Accessed January 15, 2018. https://www.
    psychologytoday.com/us/.

9   Boxer, Elisa. 2017. "Here's how to conquer your fear
    according to science and Yoda." *Inc.com*. 13 December.
    Accessed December 30, 2017. https://www.inc.
    com/elisa-boxer/heres-how-to-conquer-your-fea
    r-according-to-science-and-yoda.html.

10 Tsaousides, Theo. 2015. "Is It Time to Face Your
    Biggest Fears?" *Psychology Today*. 5 November.
    Accessed January 15, 2018. https://www.
    psychologytoday.com/us/.

11   —2018. "How to Conquer Fear of Failure."
     Psychology Today. 23 January. Accessed February
     1, 2018. https://www.psychologytoday.com/
     us/blog/smashing-the-brainblocks/201801/
     how-conquer-fear-failure.

12   Ibid.

13   Kronick, Richard. 2017. "10 Powerful Ways
     Successful People Overcome Fear." *Huffington
     Post, Life*. 11 October. Accessed October 12,
     2018. https://www.huffpost.com/entry/10
     -powerful-ways-successful-people-overcome-
     fear_b_12414162.

14   Canfield, Jack. 1996. "Dare to Win." In *Dare to Win*,
     by Jack and Hansen Canfield.

15   McCracken, Mareo. 2018. "This Neuroscience
     Trick will Help You Overcome any fear." *Inc.
     com*. 29 January. Accessed February 15, 2018.
     https://www.inc.com/mareo-mccracken/
     this-neuroscience-trick-will-help-yo
     u-overcome-any-fear.html?cid=nl029week05day29.

16   — 2018. "The only thing you need to do to overcome
     fear according to neuroscience." *Thrive Global.com*.
     16 March. Accessed August 1, 2018. https://www.
     thriveglobal.com/stories/the-only-thing-you-need-t
     o-do-to-overcome-fear-according-to-neuroscience/
     McCracken, Mareo, March 16, 2018.

17   Ibid.

18   Simmons, Russell. 2010. "Marie Forleo." *marieforleo.
     com*. June. Accessed January 2, 2018. https://www.
     marieforleo.com/2010/06/feel-failure-good/.

Step three — Why franchising?

1   International Franchise Association - IFA. 2018. *What
     are common franchise terms?* Accessed April 10, 2018.
     https://www.franchise.org/what-are-common-franchis
     e-terms.

2   WebFinance, Inc. 2018. "franchising. BusinessDictionary.com." *WebFinance, Inc.* Accessed October 1, 2018. http://www.businessdictionary.com/definition/franchising.html.

3   Seid, Michael. 2017. "The History of Franchising." *"The Balance: Small Business"*. MSA Worldwide. 13 April. Accessed January 26, 2018. https://www.thebalance.com/the-history-of-franchising-1350455.

4   Ibid.

5   International Franchise Association - IFA. 2018. "What is a franchise?" *Franchise.org.* Accessed October 8, 2018. https://www.franchise.org/what-is-a-franchise.

6   Oswald, Cherie. 2016. *Accenture, LLP.* 24 June . Accessed October 2, 2018. https://www.accenture.com/us-en/blogs/blogs-be-your-own-harry-potter.

7   Oxford University Press. 2018. *Oxford Dictionary.* Accessed 3 10, 2017. https://en.oxforddictionaries.com/definition/franchise.

8   PwC. "The Economic Impact of Franchised Businesses: Volume IV, 2016." *Franchise.org.* September 15, 2016. Accessed December 15, 2017. https://www.franchise.org/sites/default/files/Economic%20Impact%20of%20Franchised%20Businesses_Vol%20IV_20160915.pdf.

9   Judy, Jim. 2018. "Choosing a Hot Franchise May Leave You Cold." *Entrepreneur.com.* 11 February. Accessed February 15, 2018. https://www.entrepreneur.com/article/307708.

10 Salario, Alizah. 2016. "Are you fit to own a franchise?" *Metro.us.* Metro US. 26 June. Accessed November 20, 2017. https://www.metro.us/lifestyle/are-you-fit-to-own-a-franchise/zsJpfq---AUdvAMfY91oQg.

11 Ibid.

12 Sugars, Brad. 2018. "Follow the System." *Franchisehelp.com.* Accessed January 15, 2018. https://

www.franchisehelp.com/franchisee-resource-center/
follow-the-system/.

13 Templeman, Mike. 2014. "Starting a Business: 20
    Reasons to Start Your Own Business." *Entrepreneur.
    com.* 20 June. Accessed May 15, 2017. https://www.
    entrepreneur.com/article/234916).

14 *Columbus Business First.* Buchanan, Doug, ed. 2018.
    Accessed May 15, 2018. https://www.bizjournals.com/
    columbus/.

15 Templeman, Mike. 2014. "Starting a Business: 20
    Reasons to Start Your Own Business." *Entrepreneur.
    com.* 20 June. Accessed May 15, 2017. https://www.
    entrepreneur.com/article/234916).

16 TenBrook, Keith. 2009-2018. "Decision timing - How
    to get it right and prevent major decision traps."
    Decision Innovation.com. Edited by Gary DeGregorio.
    Accessed December 2, 2017. https://www.
    decision-making-solutions.com/decision-timing.html.

17 Williams, Nancy. 2018. "The perfect franchise for this
    retired nfl athlete." *Black Enterprise.com.* 25 March.
    Accessed May 15, 2018. http://www.blackenterprise.
    com/the-perfect-franchise-for-this-retire
    d-nfl-athlete/.

18 Jefferson, Tafa. Interview by Trish Benedik. 2018.
    Athlete to Franchisor (20 December).

19 Bates, Cindy. 2014. "Talk this week with Veterans
    who own businesses." *Americassbdc.org.* 7 November.
    Accessed August 15, 2017. https://americassbdc.org/
    talk-this-week-with-veterans-who-own-businesses/ .

20 United States Small Business Administration. 2018.
    "About the SBA." *sba.gov.* Accessed January 3,
    2019. https://www.sba.gov/about-sba/what-we-do/
    resource-guides.

21 IFA. International Franchise Association. 2019.
    "About VetFran." *vetfran.com.* Accessed January
    3, 2019. https://www.vetfran.com/about-vetfran/
    mission/.

22 Sugars, Brad. 2018. "Follow the System." *Franchisehelp.com*. Accessed January 15, 2018. https://www.franchisehelp.com/franchisee-resource-center/follow-the-system/.

23 Rafsky, Steven M. 2008. "The Benefits of System Wide Continuity." *Franchise.org*. February. Accessed January 15, 2018. https://www.franchise.org/the-benefits-of-system-wide-continuity.

Step Four—Select a Franchise

1 TenBrook, Keith. 2018. "Decision Innovation." *Decision Making Solutions.com*. Edited by Gary DeGregorio. Accessed February 20, 2018. https://www.decision-making-solutions.com/.

2 Tsaousides, Theo. 2015. "Is It Time to Face Your Biggest Fears?" *Psychology Today*. 5 November. Accessed January 15, 2018. https://www.psychologytoday.com/us/.

3 Ibid.

4 American Heritage® Dictionary of the English Language, Fifth Edition. S.v. "pioneer.". 2016. "pioneer." Vers. Fifth Edition. *The Free Dictionary.com*. Accessed February 2, 2017. https://www.thefreedictionary.com/pioneer.

5 Powell, Terry. 2009. "8 franchise ownership myths." *Entrepreneur.com*. 3 April. Accessed 10 2018, January. https://www.entrepreneur.com/article/202898.

6 *Due diligence*. 12 October. Accessed October 23, 2018. https://en.wikipedia.org/wiki/Due_diligence.

7 Lanard, Nancy. 2017. "What is a Franchise Earnings Claim?" *Lanard and Associates.com*. 11 December. Accessed October 23, 2018. https://lanardandassociates.com/franchise-earnings-claim/.

8 Government Publishing Office. 2018. "Electronic Code of Federal Regulations." *Federal Trade Commission (FTC)*. 22 October. Accessed October 23,

2018. https://www.ecfr.gov/cgi-bin/text-idx?SID=16b
072265f66809d05e91d01775a1971&mc=true&node=s
p16.1.436.c&rgn=div6.

Step Five — Making a Decision

[1]   TenBrook, Keith. 2018. "Decision Making Solutions." *Decision Innovation.com.* Edited by Gary
DeGregorio. Accessed February 20, 2018.
http://www.decision-making-solutions.com/
decision-making-in-uncertainty.html.

[2]   LaVallo, Dan and Oliver Sibony. 2016. "Early
Stage Research on Decision Making Styles."
McKinsey.com. April. Accessed January 10, 2018.
https://www.mckinsey.com/business-functions/
strategy-and-corporate-finance/our-insights/
early-stage-research-on-decision-making-styles).

[3]   Ibid.

[4]   Sherman, Erik. 2013. "Which of the 5 kinds
of decision maker are you?" *Inc.com.* 30 April.
Accessed December 10, 2017. https://www.inc.
com/erik-sherman/which-of-the-5-kinds-o
f-decision-maker-are-you.html.

[5]   Ibid.

[6]   Ibid.

[7]   Ibid.

[8]   Ibid.

[9]   LaVallo, Dan and Oliver Sibony. 2016. "Early
Stage Research on Decision Making Styles."
McKinsey.com. April. Accessed January 10, 2018.
https://www.mckinsey.com/business-functions/
strategy-and-corporate-finance/our-insights/
early-stage-research-on-decision-making-styles).

[10]   TenBrook, Keith. 2018. "Decision Innovation."
Decision Making Solutions.com. Edited by Gary
DeGregorio. Accessed February 20, 2018. https://
www.decision-making-solutions.com/.

11   UMASS/Dartmouth. 2018. ""Decision-Making
      Process." How to Get Good Grades- UMass
      Dartmouth." *University of Massachusetts Dartmouth.*
      Accessed February 20, 2018. https://www.umassd.edu/
      fycm/decisionmaking/process/.

12   Gray, Kescia D. 2014-2015. "5 Steps to Good
      Decision Making." *corporatewellnessmagazine.*
      com. Accessed July 15, 2018. https://www.
      corporatewellnessmagazine.com/focuse
      d/5-steps-to-good-decision-making/.

13   Stangler, Dane. 2009. *Research reports and covers.*
      Research, Kansas City, MO: Ewing Marion
      Kauffman Foundation. Accessed December
      12, 2017. https://www.kauffman.org/-/media/
      kauffman_org/research-reports-and-covers/2009/06/
      theeconomicfuturejusthappened.pdf.

14   Opportunity cost. *businessdictionary.com.* Accessed
      December 15, 2016. http://www.businessdictionary.
      com/definition/opportunity-cost.html.

15   TenBrook, Keith. 2018. "Decision Making
      Solutions." *Decision Innovation.com.* Edited by
      Gary DeGregorio. Accessed February 20, 2018.
      http://www.decision-making-solutions.com/
      decision-making-in-uncertainty.html.

16   Godin, Seth. 2018. *Blog: Difficult Decisions.* 11 August.
      https://seths.blog/2018/08/difficult-decisions/.

Step Six — Running your Business

1   Blake, Aaron. 2012. "Obama's 'You didn't build that'
      problem." *WashingtonPost.com.* 12 July. Accessed January-
      ary 4, 2017. https://www.washingtonpost.com/blogs/
      the-fix/post/obamas-you-didnt-build-that-proble
      m/2012/07/18/gJQAJxyotW_blog.
      html?utm_term=.09851a46c80d.

2   Obront, Zach. 2017. "13 life rules to keep you
      motivated." *Success.com.* 21 April. Accessed

January 15, 2018. https://www.success.
com/13-life-rules-to-keep-you-motivated/.

3   Cardone, Grant. 2016. "Are you 9 to 5 or 95?"
     Medium.com. 29 November. Accessed January
     15, 2018. https://medium.com/@grantcardone/
     are-you-9-to-5-or-95-fbbe844ae733.

4   Elkins, Kathleen. 2016. *cnbc.com.* 5 12. Accessed
     12 28, 2017. (Elkins, https://www.cnbc.
     com/2016/12/05/self-made-millionaire-if-you-wan
     t-to-get-rich-start-working-95-hours-a-week.html).

5   Cardone, Grant. 2016. "Are you 9 to 5 or 95?"
     Medium.com. 29 November. Accessed January
     15, 2018. https://medium.com/@grantcardone/
     are-you-9-to-5-or-95-fbbe844ae733.

6   Boehle, Steven. 2017. "5 reasons why starting
     your own business is hard." *cobound.co.* 1
     December. Accessed January 15, 2018. https://
     cobound.co/5-reasons-why-starting-your-ow
     n-business-is-hard.

7   Ibid.

8   Harris, Joshua. 2017. "The Best Advice these 11
     successful people ever received." *Theoracles.com.* 23
     July. Accessed November 15, 2017. https://articles.
     theoracles.com/the-best-advice-these-11-successfu
     l-people-ever-received-81b5d31febe1.

9   Sandler Training. 1999-2018. *Sandler International.*
     Accessed January 15, 2018. https://www.sandler.com/.

10   Cuban, Mark. 2008. *blogmaverick.* 9 March.
     Accessed January 15, 2018. http://blogmaverick.
     com/2008/03/09/my-rules-for-startups/.

11   Roberge, Matt. 2016. "I Finally Understand
     Why Most Small Businesses Don't Succeed."
     Huffingtonpost.com. 6 July. Accessed November 15,
     2017. https://www.huffingtonpost.com/matt-roberg
     e/i-finally-understand-why-_b_10734126.html.

12   Bigby, Garenne. 2018. "Top 25 freelance
     websites to find work in 2018." *Dynomapper.*

com. 17 October. Accessed October 31, 2018. https://dynomapper.com/blog/266-top-25-fre elance-websites-to-find-work-in-2018.

13 Frost, Aja. 2018. "The 23 Most Highly-Rated Sales Books of All Time." *Hubspot.com*. Accessed November 1, 2018. https://blog.hubspot.com/sales/ the-most-highly-rated-sales-books-of-all-time.

14 *Audible.com*. Accessed January 5, 2018. https://www. audible.com/.

15 Borja, Chris, interview by Trish Benedik. 2018. *Fear of Networking* (30 July).

16 *Meetup.com*. Accessed January 15, 2017. https://www. meetup.com/.

17 *Lions International*. Accessed April 30, 2018. https:// lionsclubs.org/

18 *Rotary.org*. Accessed April 15, 2018. https://www. rotary.org/.

19 *Kiwanis.org*. Accessed 15 2018, August. https://www. kiwanis.org/.

20 *AmSpirit Business Connections*. Accessed August 15, 2018. https://www.amspirit.com/.

21 *Business Networking International, BNI Global, LLC*. Accessed August 15, 2018. https://www.bni.com/.

22 *Toastmasters.org*. Accessed August 15, 2018. https:// www.toastmasters.org/.

23 *SCORE.org*. Accessed January 15, 2018. https://www. score.org/.

24 Salario, Alizah. 2016. "Are you fit to own a franchise?" *Metro.us*. Metro US. 26 June. Accessed November 20, 2017. https://www.metro.us/ lifestyle/are-you-fit-to-own-a-franchise/ zsJpfq---AUdvAMfY91oQg.

25 Hodjat, Nafise Nina. 2017. "The best career advice from successful people who made it to the top." *Success.com*. 20 July . Accessed January 5, 2018. https://www.success.com/

article/the-best-career-advice-from-successfu
l-people-who-made-it-to-the-top.

Glossary

[1]   International Franchise Association - IFA. 2018. *What
are common franchise terms?* Accessed April 10, 2018.
https://www.franchise.org/what-are-common-franchis
e-terms.

[2]   Entrepreneur Media. 2019. "Business Opportunity."
entrepreneur.com/encylopedia. Accessed January 3,
2019. https://www.entrepreneur.com/encyclopedia/
business-opportunity.

[3]   United States Federal Trade Commission. 2018.
"Business Opportunity Rule." *ftc.gov.* Accessed
January 3, 2019. https://www.ftc.gov/enforcement/
rules/rulemaking-regulatory-reform-proceedings/
business-opportunity-rule.

[4]   Federal Trade Commission. 2018. "What we do." *ftc.
gov.* Accessed January 3, 2019. https://www.ftc.gov/
about-ftc/what-we-do.

[5]   Kenton, Will, ed. 2018. "Franchise Disclosure
Document." *Investopedia.* 1 July. Accessed January
9, 2019. https://www.investopedia.com/terms/f/
franchise-disclosure-document.asp.

[6]   —2017. "Franchise." *Investopedia.com.* 14 December.
Accessed January 10, 2019. https://www.investopedia.
com/terms/f/franchise.asp.

[7]   Franchise agreement. *BusinessDictionary.com.
Webfinance, Inc.* Accessed 10 2019, January.
http://www.businessdictionary.com/definition/
franchise-agreement.html.

[8]   Federal Trade Commission. 2018.
"Franchise Rule". Accessed January 3, 2019.
https://www.ftc.gov/enforcement/rules/
rulemaking-regulatory-reform-proceedings/
franchise-rule.

9   Franchisee. *Investopedia.com/terms*. 24 September.
     Accessed January 10, 2019. https://www.investopedia.
     com/terms/f/franchisee.asp.

10   Franchising. International Franchise Association
     - IFA. 2018. *What are common franchise terms?*
     Accessed April 10, 2018. https://www.franchise.org/
     what-are-common-franchise-terms.

11   Franchisor. International Franchise Association
     - IFA. 2018. *What are common franchise terms?*
     Accessed April 10, 2018. https://www.franchise.org/
     what-are-common-franchise-terms.

12   Product distribution franchise. International Franchise
     Association - IFA. 2018. *What are common franchise
     terms?* Accessed April 10, 2018. https://www.
     franchise.org/what-are-common-franchise-terms.

13   Royalty. International Franchise Association - IFA.
     2018. *What are common franchise terms?* Accessed
     April 10, 2018. https://www.franchise.org/
     what-are-common-franchise-terms.

14   United States Small Business Administration. 2018.
     "About the SBA." *sba.gov.* Accessed January 3,
     2019. https://www.sba.gov/about-sba/what-we-do/
     resource-guides.

15   Trademark. International Franchise Association
     - IFA. 2018. *What are common franchise terms?*
     Accessed April 10, 2018. https://www.franchise.org/
     what-are-common-franchise-terms.

16   VetFran. International Franchise Association
     - IFA. 2018. *What are common franchise terms?*
     Accessed April 10, 2018. https://www.franchise.org/
     what-are-common-franchise-terms.

ACKNOWLEDGEMENTS

My thanks

To my husband for his unwavering support and
the extra motivation to finish this book.

To my editor Brad Fruhauff, at *The Pen and Pint*,
for his outstanding insight and advice.

To my family and friends for their encouragement.

To Kary Oberbrunner and the AAE team without
whom this book would not have been written.

To my dogs Lilly and Tucker for always
being at my side.

To 99Designs and WildEagles for the
fantastic cover art.

ABOUT THE AUTHOR

Trish Benedik has a wide-ranging background in business and education. She received her Bachelor's degree in Business Administration from Franklin University and Master's Degree in Workforce Development and Education from The Ohio State University. Trish's business involvements include work in advertising and marketing and ownership of retail and wholesale businesses. She taught business courses at the high school and college level. In addition, Trish owns a multi-unit fundraising franchise and enjoys helping schools, churches, and non-profit groups with their fundraising needs. As a franchise consultant, she assists individuals in choosing franchises that are the right fit. A native of southeastern Ohio where she spent several years riding horses and competing in equestrian events; she lives near Columbus, Ohio.

Connect at trishbenedik.com

TAKE YOUR NEXT STEP

RESOLVE TO BE A FEARLESS FRANCHISEE

BOLDLY BUY OR START A BUSINESS

Live the life you imagine!

- *Let Trish walk you through the process, step-by-step.*

- *Clarify your goals, purpose, and business.*

- *Dive deeper into franchises and business options.*

- *Sign up for an introductory consultation today.*

Connect with Trish at
trishbenedik.com

CPSIA information can be obtained
at www.ICGtesting.com
Printed in the USA
FFHW011015180419
51705375-57168FF